collapse weave

Creating Three-Dimensional Cloth

Anne Field

A&C Black · London

First published in Great Britain in 2008 by

A & C Black Publishers Limited
38 Soho Square
London W1D 3HB
www.acblack.com

ISBN: 978-1-4081-0628-0

Copyright © 2008 Anne Field

CIP Catalogue records for this book are available from the British Library and
the U.S. Library of Congress.

All rights reserved. No part of this publication may be reproduced in any form or by any means – graphic, electronic, or mechanical, including photocopying, recording, taping or information storage and retrieval systems – without the prior permission in writing of the publishers.

This book is produced using paper that is made from wood grown in managed, sustainable forests. It is natural, renewable and recyclable. The logging and manufacturing processes conform to the environmental regulations of the country of origin.

Cover design by Sutchinda Thompson

Printed in Taiwan by
Sunny Young Printing Ltd

Contents

Chapter One : Background _____ 6

Yarn • Structure • End uses • Samples • Explanation of drafts used in this book • Shuttles

Chapter Two : Yarn Structure: Twist _____ 14

S and Z Twist • Yarn handle • Luster • Yarn naming • Twist and size • Summary

Chapter Three : Active and Passive Yarns _____ 24

Active yarns • Passive yarns • Using active and passive yarns • Testing yarns
• Finishing techniques • Summary

Chapter Four : Weave Structure _____ 46

3/1 and 1/3 twill • Width of stripes • Sett • Yarn size and type • Experiment
• Color sequence • Contrast areas • Structure changes in stripes • Finishing

Chapter Five : Warping and Threading the Loom _____ 66

Using a warping mill/warping board and raddle and warping from back to front
• Short warps up to 15 feet (4.5m) • Warping over 15 feet (4.5m) with two warp beams
• Warps over 15 feet (4.5m) with only one warp beam • Sectional warping

Chapter Six : Four-shaft Double Weave _____ 72

Four shaft double weave • Winding the warp • Weaving a tube, method one
• Weaving a tube, method two • Exchanging two layers • Floats • Floats in both layers
• Joining two layers with pick-up weaving

Chapter Seven : Eight- to Sixteen-shaft Double Weaves _____ 82
Eight-shaft double weave • 2/2 twill/plain weave tube • Weaving a tube in 2/2 twill joined at the selvedges • Weaving a 3/1 twill and plain weave tube joined at the selvedges • Complex eight - and twelve-shaft double weaves • Exchanging two layers in 2/2 twill • Two layers with white floats (eight shafts) • Twelve-shaft double weave • Exchanging vertical layers (eight shafts) • Plain weave layers • Reversing the layers • Separate layers with interchanges • Sixteen-shaft twill: exchanging the layers • Vertical interchange • Vertical interchange in 2/2 twill • Vertical and horizontal interchange • Separate layers joined in blocks • Supplementary warps • Supplementary warp with both layers collapsing • Supplementary warp with floats • Supplementary warp in elastic yarns

Chapter Eight : Bumps, Lumps and Spaces _____ 104
Shrinkage • Silk and wool squares • Basket weave • Deflected double weave • Tracking and felting • Gathering • Floats • Spaced warp and weft • Gathered squares

Chapter Nine : Odds and Ends _____ 124
Felted floats • Swedish Lace • Overshot Weave • Worms • Miniature Monk's belt • Italian diamond • Diagonal twill • Huckaback • Advancing twill

Chapter Ten : Projects _____ 140
Scarves • Wraps • Straight top • Mobius top • Cocoon • Pants • Skirt

Appendix _____ 150
List of Suppliers _____ 154
Bibliography _____ 156

Acknowledgements

This book has been three years in the making. When I began it I was planning a short book, the sum total of my knowledge at the time. However, as I wrote, researched and sampled I learnt so much that the book just kept growing. Three years later it has tripled in size.

This is due not only to my own curiosity but also to the support and knowledge I have gained from others. Special thanks should go to weavers Sandra Rude, USA and Sue Foulkes, UK. Their analytical minds put me right many a time and their own collapse weaving has been an inspiration.

The following weavers have also added their expertise:
Jane Clark, Win Currie, Helen Fry, Brigit Howitt, Trudy Newman, Fran Regan, Sheila Reimann and Irene Schiffer. Knitter Tracey White and fashion designer Sylvia Campbell have also added to this book. Without you it would have been a very small book indeed.

The weaving in the photographs has been woven by me, unless other weavers are credited. The photographs were taken by Edward Field, unless credited otherwise. Thanks also to Valerie and Hayward Osborn for their meticulous proof reading.

I would like to thank my husband, Edward, for his listening skills, computer support and photography expertise during those three years. We are a good team.

1 Background

For 30 years my aim was to weave fabrics that were flat and consistent. Although I varied the texture and pattern, I could tell from the appearance of the fabric on the loom what it would look like finished – usually somewhat the same only better! Several years ago I was staying with a weaver, Fran Regan, in New South Wales, Australia, and she had a most interesting wrap she had woven after seeing some wraps woven by Alan Tremain, a well-known Australian weaver. I had never seen anything like it. Over the next three days Fran spun some over-twisted handspun singles for the weft and I threaded up her loom and wove a wrap. She had to quickly spin a mighty lot of wool to get it woven in three days. I did not quite know how it worked, apart from the knowledge that the over-twisted weft pulled in the loose weave, but it intrigued me. It was the first time I had seen pleated and puckered fabric that was not an accident but done deliberately. It was my very first collapse weave cloth.

Collapse cloth is hard to define because the collapse is caused by many factors. However, these fabrics do have one feature in common: collapse cloth is flexible and fluid in movement. When it is taken from the loom and washed, the change from a rigid arrangement of threads on the loom to a cloth that bends, distorts and deviates from the usual linear movement of most other cloth is amazing. This is what makes it unique.

There are two main ways it can be woven: first by contrasting the different yarn factors, such as twist, shrinkage and size, and secondly by using weave structures that react with each other to form ridges and hollows. In other words, one type uses the properties of the yarn and the other uses the weave structure. Many collapse weaves use both.

YARN

Yarn under tension on the loom is controlled and held in straight lines by the loom frame and reed and cannot move much. When the tension is released and the fabric is washed it will change. We all know that hand weaving should be washed after it is taken from the loom, apart from some exceptions such as floor rugs and tapestries. Washing turns a structure that on the loom looks like separate warp threads crossed by weft threads into a fabric. With fulling or milling the threads mesh together to different degrees, depending on the yarn type and structure, to make a stable fabric. Moisture,

Photo 1-1. Collapse weave scarf where the collapse is caused by the yarn structure.

heat and movement are necessary in this fulling process which, carried to extremes with woolen fabrics, causes felting.

Some yarns change more in the finishing process than others do. Rayon will not change much when washed; all that happens is that it contracts slightly when the warp tension is released. Soft woolen yarn will change much more in the finishing process. Woolen yarns stretch more than rayon on the loom and the release of tension will contract the fabric. Then, with washing, the fabric shrinks. This shrinkage differs from yarn to yarn. Yarn spun from Merino sheep will shrink more than yarn from an English Leicester sheep. As a general rule, yarn from the finer wool breeds shrinks more than yarn from coarser breeds. By mixing the yarns in stripes, one stripe of rayon, for example, with one stripe of wool, or with two different types of woolen yarn, we can form pleated, puckered or seersucker fabric after washing.

Collapse Weave

Photo 1-2a. (left) Collapse weave scarf where the collapse is caused by the weave structure.
Woven by Irene Schiffer, Australia

Photo 1-2b. (below) Detail of 1.2a

We can also mix yarns that have been spun differently. When an over-twisted yarn is washed it tries to undo itself and revert back to its original form, becoming more active and pulling more passive yarns out of place into pleats and waves. An elastic yarn will pull the fabric in when the fabric is washed. Puckers and pleats formed by the structure of the yarn are less rigid in form and inclined to wave more than pleats formed by the weave structure.

STRUCTURE

We know that different weave structures react differently when removed from the loom and washed. A simple example of this is when we combine weft stripes of plain weave (over-one, under-one) with a 2/2 twill (over-two, under-two). The twill weave pulls in more than the plain weave. It is the number of intersections that makes a difference: with fewer intersections, the more the weave contracts.

The most common form of structural collapse is by combining warp stripes of 3/1 twill with 1/3 twill. If spaced correctly, 1/3 twill forms a weft-face fabric on the top

Background

Figure 1-1a. Cross section of plain weave

Figure 1-2a. Cross section of 1/3 warp with weft-emphasis stripe

Figure 1-1b. Cross section of 2/2 twill weave

Figure 1-2b. Cross section of 3/1 warp with warp-emphasis stripe

surface, with the weft going under one and over three warp threads, and the stripe will recede. The 3/1 twill stripe with the weft going under three and over one, forms a warp-face fabric on the surface and the stripe will advance. Combine these two and you will have a uniformly pleated surface. Again the fabric needs to be washed to achieve the best effect, because the yarns will contract, accentuating the weft and warp-faced stripes.

One challenge with this method of weaving pleats is that the pleats are more defined if there are more picks to the inch (ppi), than there are ends per inch (epi), which can make the structure somewhat inflexible, thus limiting the end use.

Other weave structures such as overshots and one-shuttle weaves cause different effects and these are discussed in Chapter Nine. The more I research these weaves the more there is to find and the scope is limitless.

These two types of collapse weave can be combined. For example, you can weave warp and weft-face stripes with an over-twisted or elastic yarn as a weft, which solves the problem of the inflexibility of the fabric. These types of collapse weave will be covered fully in later chapters, but it helps to understand the basic concepts at this stage. There are also many variations within these two main groups and these will be covered in later chapters. For example, the ability to spin your own yarns can add to the possibilities of the woven cloth.

Once you have an interest in a particular subject, it is odd how you find it everywhere. About two weeks after I decided to write this book, I was reading Elizabeth Wayland Barber's book The Mummies of Urumchi. There, in one of the photos, was a baby's shroud decorated with collapse weave. About every 25-30 rows there were 3-4 rows of weaving in the same yarn but overspun. It was too regular to be anything but deliberate. I can imagine that mother, grieving for her child and wanting to make the very best covering for the shroud, adorning the fabric with that pattern. Some of these mummies date back 4000 years, so what I am weaving now is not new.

Only a couple of weeks after seeing this photo, I was looking at cloth fragments in the Victoria and Albert Museum in London and saw a piece of handspun woolen cloth with an over-twisted singles yarn used as a decorative fringe.

Museums collecting textiles are not only faced with the problem of the fragile nature of cloth, but also with what to collect. Tapestries depicting great battles or other historic moments are collected; crude curtains that hung in peasant doorways are not.

Collapse Weave

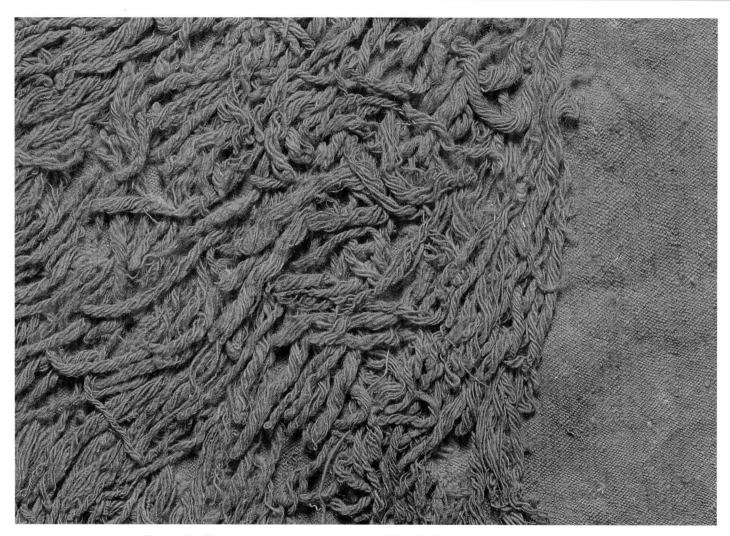

Photo 1-3. Cloth fragment of an Egyptian scarf (300-499 AD) from the Victoria and Albert Museum, London. Photo courtesy of V and A Picture library

Background

Photo 1-4. Woolen seersucker fabric

These simple fabrics were not treated with care, and were simply replaced when they disintegrated through hard wear. So museum collections consist mainly of cloth the rich would wear, brocades, silk clothing, fine linens, and the like. An exhibition of Chinese clothing in Australia recently did show the finely embroidered clothing of the rich, but it also displayed the blue cotton clothing of peasants, some of it so stitched and mended that the fabric looked like patchwork. These humble garments had much of the maker in them. I could imagine women cutting up worn out coats and making one coat out of two tattered ones, because the cloth was too precious to discard. The hand of the maker was evident in these garments in a way not seen in the rich embroidered coats because the wearers of the fancy clothing would not have made the garments that adorned them. So this simple fabric remnant in the Victoria and Albert, means more to me as a weaver and spinner, than the fine tapestries and brocade clothing of the rich.

When I began making my own clothes in the 1960s I can well remember a seersucker fabric I made into a dress. Now I can weave my own seersucker by adding at regular intervals one or two warp ends that will shrink and pucker the fabric when it is wet finished. The wool bouclé used as the active yarn in Photo 1.4 was some yarn I bought 20 or more years ago, then could not use because it shrank about a third of its length when washed. This does prove the benefit of collecting yarn, even when you can see no use for it at the time.

Cloth needs to be flexible to be made into comfortable clothing, curtains, coverings, towels and the many other textiles we surround ourselves with. And by utilizing the flexibility of cloth we can weave it into fabrics that flow, pleat and pucker at will. New fibers are constantly coming on the market and the different properties of these fibers, when understood and utilized properly, can lead to many exciting effects. The new machine-washable, non-shrinkable wool, when woven with wool yarn that shrinks, can produce interesting fabric, and is just one of the many new processes that can be used by the weaver to make highly original fabric.

This book will explain how to make many of these fabrics and will also show some finished cloth to inspire you to try this fascinating weave for itself. It is not a structure, it is not a pattern. It does not fit into any of the types of weaves we are familiar with but it makes use of a truth we sometimes forget while weaving – that cloth is a flexible structure.

Yarns that are suitable for collapse weave are becoming easier to find. Initially I had to spin all my over-twisted yarns, or find yarn rejected from mills because of over-twist. This limited the amount of weaving that could be done. Gradually the availability of suitable yarns increased and now some are being especially spun for us. Although the range is wider, it is still limited. I have included a suppliers list at the end of the book and the yarns used in the samples in this book are mostly from that list. Over the years I have been weaving collapse fabrics I have been collecting odd yarns. Some are given to me because other weavers have no use for them and some I have persuaded small mills to spin for me. Where the yarn used in the woven samples is not in the suppliers list I have included in the weaving instructions a description of the yarn, and the size in wraps per inch. This is a reasonably accurate method of measuring yarn by wrapping it around a ruler for an inch so the strands are touching. Then count the number of strands.

END USES

The end use of collapse weave cloth is determined by the structure. To give a ridiculous example, there would be no point in making a tweed-type jacket from this type of cloth. The beauty of collapse weave is that it produces a light, flexible cloth that drapes well. When I began weaving collapse weave I made only scarves. This is an ideal place to start, and the length-wise pleating makes this fabric perfect for scarves. As I became more knowledgeable and adventurous, I began to make tops and pants. I also found a very imaginative fashion designer, and we began to branch out into garments and wearable art, some of which can be seen in the color photographs.

The handle of the cloth is probably the most important feature of collapse fabric. To utilize the drape and movement of collapse fabric, some yarns are better than others. I have seen beautiful looking fabrics that are harsh to touch and could not be worn next to the skin. That is why this book concentrates on fine wool yarns, because most wool yarn can be over-twisted and still retain the soft, flexible nature that we desire. Some cottons, silks and Lycra yarns are also soft and flexible enough but it pays to test yarns first.

Once you have seen what can be done with the samples and have some knowledge of the finished size of the fabric compared to the loom measurements, try some of the projects in the last chapter. These are just suggestions to get started. I spend a lot of waiting time at the dentist or hairdresser looking at fashion magazines. Some very good

SAMPLES

The first five chapters of this book discuss the causes of collapse weave. To demonstrate what happens I have included samples to weave to help in the understanding of these basic principles. These samples will be separated from the text and will use the same warp and weft yarn unless otherwise stated. My understanding of weave structures comes more from weaving than from reading, and I know from my teaching experience over many years that many weavers are the same. So put on the warp described on page 17, Sample A and weave as you read. Some are for a four-shaft loom, some for an eight-shaft and some can be woven on either. If you have an eight-shaft loom, there are more complex techniques you can weave. Chapters Six, Seven, Eight and Nine will expand this knowledge by discussing different weave structures, with accompanying photographs and drafts.

---

ideas can be had from such magazines and by adapting and modifying ideas seen there we can design our own collapse weave garments. Remember that flat areas can contrast with the collapse areas so only part of a garment can be woven in collapse weave.

I think my fascination with collapse weaves is that for the first time my spinning and weaving knowledge have come together. My knowledge of the count and direction of twist in handspun yarn, together with different yarn properties, learnt over 40 years of hand spinning, and added to my weaving skills, can produce unique fabrics that industrial looms would be hard pressed to emulate. And it is such fun. On the loom I can weave something that looks like badly woven netting. When washed it becomes a soft, pliable fabric that bounces and moves with the wearer.

EXPLANATION OF DRAFTS USED IN THIS BOOK

In this book I have assumed that readers have some basic weaving knowledge, are familiar with commonly used weaving terms and can read drafts. Many of the weave structures are plain weaves or twills and are not complex.

The software used for the drafts in this book is AVL's Weavepoint 6.1. Many of the drafts have been modified to show the yarns used in the warp and the weft. The threading draft is in the top left quadrant and reads from right to left, beginning with Shaft 1 in the lower right hand corner. The tie-up is in the top right quadrant. The treadling drafts (bottom right quadrant) reads from top to bottom. In the draw-downs (bottom left quadrant) a black square represents a warp end on the surface of the weaving.

SHUTTLES

Collapse weave mainly uses elastic or over-twisted yarn as the weft. Using an end-delivery shuttle is the best way to straighten the weft crossing through the shed, as it adds drag to the yarn.

2 Yarn Structure : Twist

It is necessary to learn about the structure of yarn in order to understand why collapse happens. The most important factor when discussing collapse fabrics is the twist of the yarn. There are several other reasons why fabric will pleat and pucker, and usually one or more of these is contained in one piece of fabric, but the twist seems to hold the secret in most collapse cloth. Twist is probably more important when weaving collapse fabric based on the yarn structure alone, but it also has its place when weaving fabrics where the collapse is caused by the weaving structure.

Fibers are twisted together in the spinning process to make yarn strong because untwisted fibers are generally weak and break easily. Fine yarn needs more twist than thicker yarn because it requires added strength. However, twisting unbalances the yarn because twist is added in one direction only, making an active yarn. If you twist a yarn then let go it will unwind as the fibers try to return to their original state. If the two ends of a singles yarn are held together, the yarns will twist around each other in the opposite direction, again trying to return to their original state. This is the reason why many yarns are plied, that is two or more strands of singles yarn are twisted or folded together in the opposite direction to balance them. If the twist in the singles is balanced with the twist in the plying, the twist is neutralized, the fibers run straight for the length of the yarn and the yarn is strong and stable. When hand spinning, a balanced yarn is made by plying two singles together with two thirds of the twist of the singles and in the opposite direction. When plying in the opposite direction, some of the original twist is undone, then more opposing twist added, hence the two thirds proportion. If the plying adds too much or too little twist, the yarn will still be unbalanced. When using the term 'over-twisted' I refer to yarns that do not have the fibers running parallel, and are therefore unbalanced. The degree of over-twist can vary greatly.

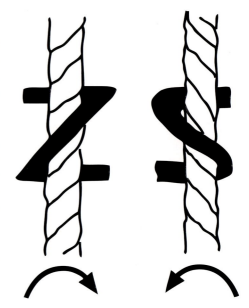

Figure 2-1. S and Z twist in yarn

S AND Z TWIST

For years I had problems remembering which direction the yarn twisted while I was spinning. An easy way is to look at the top of the letters. To begin drawing the letter Z, your hand moves from left to right. To begin the letter S, your hand moves from right to left. When spinning the wheel moves in the same direction, in other words, with a Z twist yarn the wheel is moving in a clockwise direction, with an S twist yarn in an

Photo 2-1. Scarf woven with inch stripes of S and Z singles spun yarn

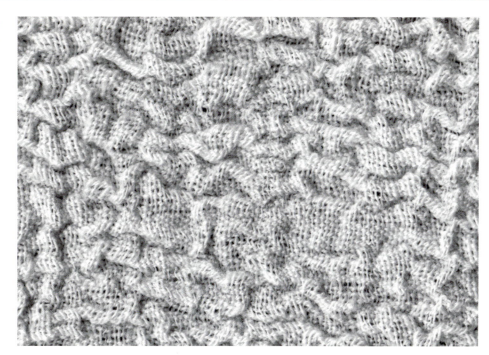

anti-clockwise direction. Most of the spinners in the classes I have taught spin the singles Z and then ply in an S direction. This is also the same way most of the commercially plied yarns I use in weaving are twisted. Whether that is related or just coincidence, I do not know.

When I was studying commercial yarns to see in which direction they twisted I decided to test the qualities of yarns with an opposing twist. Because the commercial yarns I had available to me had the same direction of twist, I had to do this on my spinning wheel. I spun one bobbin of singles Z twist and another bobbin of S twist. It was not easy spinning the S singles because I have spent 40 years spinning my handspun singles clockwise with a Z twist. Every time I sat at the spinning wheel for the S bobbin I had to continually remind myself to turn the wheel anti-clockwise. In Photo 2-1 the weft was a

Collapse Weave

Photo 2-2a. Warp Z, weft S. Incompatible   Photo 2-2b. Warp S, weft S. Compatible

commercial 110/2 yarn, spun in an S direction, but the warp has one-inch stripes of the S and Z spun yarn. The weave structure was plain weave. An explanation on yarn naming is on page 22. Handspinning is covered in some detail in the appendix.

The difference in the S-twist stripe to the Z-twist stripe is noticeable: one curves upwards, the other downwards, with an interesting little spiral where the two stripes meet. This change in appearance is also caused by the different light reflection on the S-twist stripe compared to the Z-twist stripe. It can be seen that weaving collapse fabrics changes many of our normal weaving habits, which makes it much more fun and interesting. In the appendix I will describe how to warp and thread the loom with singles yarn.

It has long been known that the direction of twist makes a difference to the behavior of yarn when woven. When warp and weft are twisted in opposite directions as in Photo 2-2a, with a Z-warp end and a S-weft pick, they appear on the surface to bed into each

Yarn Structure: Twist

Photograph A

SAMPLE A

The sample warp is 11in (28cm) wide and 15ft (4.6m) long. The warp is of two different types of yarn, a thicker wool, 110/2 Tex (for a description of the Tex system see page 22) for the first inch, sett at 16 epi. The alternate stripe is a thinner, over-twisted wool, 56/2, sett at 24 epi. The source of these yarns is in the list of suppliers, page 154. These yarns can be exchanged for others of a similar character, although the effect will be slightly different. The 110/2 is a soft shrinkable wool, labeled 'S' in the sample drafts. Another shrinkable fine wool could be used. The 56/2, labeled "O" in the drafts, is the very fine over-twisted wool. It can be exchanged for a similar over-twisted wool, or rayon. I have tried weaving with an over-twisted silk, but the handle is far too harsh, even after washing.

Drafts for both a four-shaft and an eight-shaft loom are given. The thicker yarn is in the outside two stripes to give stability. There will be six stripes of the 110/2 and five stripes of the 56/2 yarn. Each sample should be woven at least 12in (30cm) long, and beaten at 16 ppi to get the collapse effect. This sample is woven in a 2/2 twill because this structure has double the intersections of a plain weave, allowing the yarns to move and collapse.

Results when washed

The 110/2 (S) wool stripe in the warp shrinks slightly, pulling up the 56/2 (O) stripes into gentle waves. The 56/2 is passive in this warp but active in the weft, where it pulls in the fabric across the width, leaving strong vertical collapse after washing. Washing instructions are on page 43.

Collapse Weave

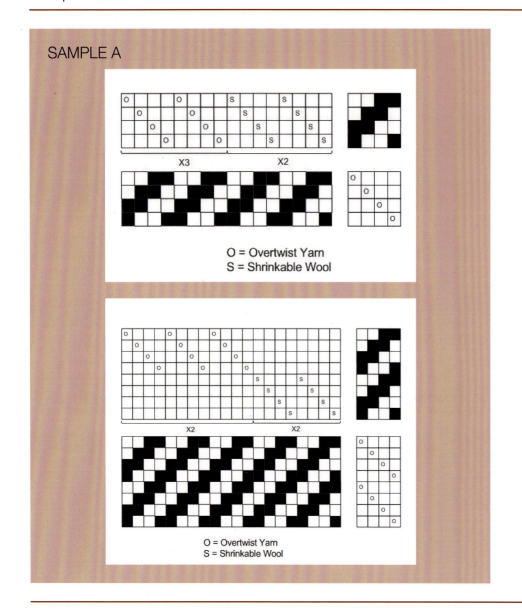

SAMPLE A

Yarn Structure: Twist

other when crossed at right angles because the angle of twist looks compatible. But the underside of the top warp end is actually angled in the opposite direction, so where it crosses the weft, the angles are incompatible. If the warp and weft twist angle is the same, as in Photo 2-2b, where both warp and weft are S twisted, the underside of the top warp end angles in the opposing direction and is compatible with the weft. The resulting fabric is thinner and more stable than if the warp and weft are twisted in the opposite direction. So what you see on the surface is not what happens where the underside of one crosses the upper side of the other. Confusing, is it not!

When weaving collapse fabric, we want the yarns to move after weaving and washing, therefore this bedding-in of yarns is not helpful. A Z-twist warp yarn crossed by an S-twist weft will move more, (or an S warp crossed by a Z weft) because they will give opposing angles, thus aiding the collapse. This point is often academic because we do not have much choice with commercial yarns which, as I stated earlier, are usually plied S.

Hanging 'Ashes'.
Woven and photographed by
Trudy Newman, Australia.
Feltable wool and silk with supplementary
warp of colored wool.

Collapse Weave

Wrap. 'Blues in the Night'.
Woven by Fran Regan, Australia.
Wool, singles and plied, bouĉle and mohair, dyed with fibre reactive dyes.
Photographer Barry Regan

    For a flat fabric a balanced yarn is used, that is one with no twist in either direction. In a collapse weave fabric some of the yarn can be over twisted. If allowed enough space the over-twisted portions, when relaxed and washed, will try to move back to their untwisted state, forming corkscrews, bumps and pleats. These active sections usually need to be contained by more stable, passive areas of yarn. If not, the complete fabric will roll and bunch, producing interesting shapes and textures but generally with not enough stability to make usable fabric. It should also be noted that the edges of collapse fabrics, where more movement is possible, have more noticeable collapse. This is the reason why most of my collapse fabrics are no wider than 21in (54cm) on the loom. If I want wider fabrics I join them. Joins are no problem with these wavy and bumpy fabrics because the join is indistinguishable.

Yarn Structure: Twist

YARN HANDLE

Twisting the yarn not only makes it stronger but also makes it feel harder. You can see this when you unwind a plied yarn. It is always softer than the original. When using wool the breed should have fine, soft wool to begin with, if you want to weave fabric that will be worn close to the skin. I am lucky that in New Zealand we have some very fine micron Merinos, some as fine as 12.5 microns. A micron is an abbreviated form of the word micrometer, one millionth of a meter, and is used to judge the fiber size. The lower the micron, the finer and softer the fiber will be. Even when spun commercially with very high twist, a low micron wool will result in soft yarn. But a high-twist yarn, spun from a coarser wool fleece such as Romney, will result in a yarn that is too harsh to wear next to the skin.

In yarns such as silk and cotton, the twist count can vary considerably, but does not appear to make such a difference in the softness of the yarn as it does with wool. Over-twisted plied yarns or unbalanced singles are available in most cottons and silks and can be used with collapse weaves although wool appears to give the best results because of its soft handle and its ability to change considerably with washing. It is just a matter of hunting these unusual yarns out. When I first began experimenting with collapse weave many years ago, I occasionally found factory rejects that were perfect for my purposes. The factory usually just gave them to me, no doubt thinking I was very odd to even want them. The yarn suppliers listed at the end should be some help, and, as most of these are very fine yarns, ordering them by mail will cost you very little in freight. A little yarn goes a long way.

Yarns can have twist added on the spinning wheel, a slow process (discussed in the appendix) but one I used before I found sources of commercial over-twisted yarns. Because of the wide range of fine wool yarns available in New Zealand, I use a lot of wool in my collapse fabrics, often mixed with silk yarns. These yarns will also be the main focus of the photographs in this book, but other yarns can be substituted.

Calculating Twist

Over-twisted yarns are those in which the fibers within the strand do not lie straight in the length of the yarn. It is difficult to calculate by eye the twist count with the fine yarn used in most collapse weaving. With singles yarns it is impossible. Even with a magnifying glass I cannot count the number of twists in the yarns I use for collapse weaving. The amount of twist is not shown on most commercial yarn packages either. However, when

Dress and bodice, woven by Anne Field, New Zealand. Seersucker, 100% wool. Photograph Edward Field.

hand spinning yarn, counting the number of twists per inch (cm) is useful and practical. The size of the yarn also makes the amount of twist variable. What is high twist in a thick yarn will be a very low twist in a fine yarn.

Measuring the angle of twist is an accurate way of determining twist count because the angle is the same whatever the thickness of the yarn. A yarn with a twist angle of 15° has much less twist than a yarn with a 45° angle, whatever the size. But again the fineness of the yarns used in collapse weave makes this angle difficult to see without very high magnification. If we all had ready access to microscopes we could use this method of calculating twist. The answer lies in practical testing of the yarns by steaming, as seen on page 41.

LUSTER

The more twist put into a yarn, the more spiral the fibers and the less luster. These fibers do not reflect light as well as if the fibers were running parallel down the straight length of the yarn.

YARN NAMING

Many yarn suppliers label their over-twisted yarns 'crepe' and these can be singles or plied, so this is a useful guide when buying yarn for collapse weave. Singles yarns are always unbalanced to some extent, depending on the amount of twist added, but they may be too weak for a warp thread.

Yarns are labeled different ways in different countries but the most common naming system tells you the number of plies and the yarn size. New Zealand wool yarns use an international metric system called Tex, which has the size first and the plies second, separated by a slash. This system describes yarns by the weight in grams per 1000 meters. 110/2 is a good example. The 110 is the size of the yarn and indicates that 1000 meters will weigh 110 grams. The 2 indicates it is a two-ply yarn. Therefore 110/2 means that two singles yarns are plied together and the combined yarn weighs 110gms per 1000 meters. In other countries other systems may be used, making it difficult for weavers, but the Tex system is becoming universal. The lower the size number, the finer the yarn.

Sometimes the order is reversed with the ply number first. It is easy to tell which number is which, because the ply number is smaller than the size number. Another example of a yarn I have used is a 1/30 yarn from Habu Textiles in the States, who also use the Tex system for their wool yarns. This is a singles yarn with a very high twist and is much finer than the 110/2. The 1 indicates it is a single strand, and the size is 30.

For my collapse fabrics, I generally go no higher than 110/2 because thicker yarns are usually not flexible enough. The singles yarns are usually spun with more twist than the plied yarns, because this is necessary for strength. This makes them ideal for collapse weaving. The yarns I have used in the samples are named in the suppliers list at the end, using names similar to the ones in the suppliers' own catalogues.

TWIST AND SIZE

The twist and the size of the yarn are closely related. A thick yarn cannot have as much twist added as a fine yarn. This is a help to weavers wanting collapse, because the thinner yarns give the flexibility required and can hold the amount of over-twist needed. The over twist also makes the yarn unstable when not under tension, which is what is needed, but special techniques are necessary to handle the yarn in its relaxed state while you are warping, beaming and threading the loom. These will be covered in a later chapter.

Over twist increases the strength of the yarn up to a certain point but after this the yarn weakens. The weaker yarns may only be suitable for weft. Test by pulling a length of yarn over your thumbnail. If it breaks easily it is not suitable for a warp yarn, unless you are a very patient weaver and good at mending breaks.

Highly twisted yarns have a lot of stretch because the twisting process shortens the yarn. Under tension on the loom, these yarns will lengthen, then contract again when the tension is released. This is very useful factor when aiming for collapse fabrics.

SUMMARY

Factors when selecting over-twisted yarns for collapse weave are:
- Direction of twist – S or Z
- Hard or soft handle.
- The amount of twist.
- Twist relative to the size of the yarn.

3 Active and Passive Yarns

Two or more types of contrasting yarns are needed to make collapse fabric. The terminology for describing these contrasting yarns differs amongst weavers. Some label yarns energized and non-energized, and others balanced and unbalanced. For ease of understanding, in this book I will label them active and passive.

Elastic types of yarn are active and there are other factors that can cause activity in yarn. Yarn can be over-twisted in the spinning process and it can shrink when washed. Passive yarns are those that will change little when taken off the loom or with washing, such as rayon or linen. The size of the yarn also makes a difference because thinner yarns are more flexible than thicker ones.

ACTIVE YARNS

Shrinkage

Yarns that shrink a lot are active. Shrinkage is caused by the yarn swelling when moisture is added. As the yarn increases in size, it contracts in length. Wool shrinks more than most other yarns, which is why it is particularly suitable for collapse weaves. The rate of shrinkage is caused by many factors. In wool, the breed is important. Shorter, finer wool such as Merino shrinks more than long-stapled wool such as English Leicester. I once wove a throw in handspun yarn, with 4-6in (10-15cm) wide stripes of Corriedale and English Leicester in the warp and weft. The white Corriedale stripes shrank much more than the coarser English Leicester, and the complete throw had bumps in the English Leicester areas. Corriedale is a half Merino breed, hence the high shrinkage rate. With handspun wool, a spinner and weaver usually knows the breed, but with commercial yarns it is more difficult.

Another guide is in the micron size of the wool fiber. The lower the micron the more the fiber will shrink. Many fleeces bought by the hand spinner will be labeled with the micron size, and this can be an accurate guide to shrinkage. The appendix covers handspun wool in more detail.

How the yarn is spun also makes a difference. Worsted spun yarn, with parallel fibers close together, shrinks less than a fluffy woolen yarn where the fibers lie in different directions and are less compressed. Worsted yarns are also generally spun from longer-staple, coarse fiber fleeces. Woolen yarns, on the other hand, are usually spun from the shorter-staple, finer breeds. Worsted yarns have a well-defined twist compared to woolen

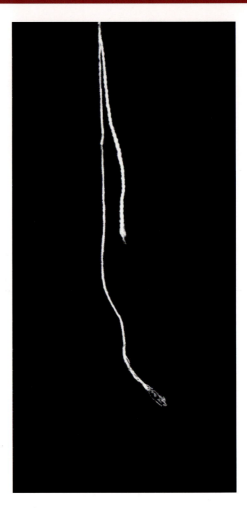

Photo 3-1. Shrinkage. 4 in (10cm) difference between rayon and wool.

Photo 3-2a. Tracking. Cotton fabric before and after washing. Sett 10 epi in 8/6 cotton. Courtesy of the Mishler Weaving Mill, Smithville, Ohio, USA.

yarns, and this can help the collapse effect. This means that worsted and woolen yarns will produce different types of collapse. In waffle weave, for example, (Photo 4-1) I prefer a woolen yarn for the long floats outlining the squares, because this helps them to felt slightly into the surface, and the floats will not catch and pull. Also the shrinkage factor will cause the floats to contract and define the deeper cells in between.

All wool, unless it has been processed to make it non-shrinkable, will shrink to a varying degree. Cotton usually shrinks less than wool, particularly if it is mercerized. Linen does not shrink. Tussah silk shrinks more than cultivated silk, and is more elastic. Most of the synthetic yarns, such as acrylic, nylon, etc. do not shrink much, but make excellent contrasting, passive yarns. Tencel (trade name Lyocell) and rayon do not shrink much.

Testing for shrinkage is simple. Take a measured, unstretched length of yarn 2-3 yards (meters) long and soak it in boiling water while agitating it with a spoon. Then

Collapse Weave

Photo 3-2b. Tracking. Warp and weft singles alpaca, very loosely woven.

rinse it in cold water. Untangle it (the hardest part) and hang up to dry. Then measure it again. To measure the relative shrinkage of two yarns, I knot them together at one end, measure them out to exactly the same length, then wash as before. When dry I can compare the different lengths. A difference of about 4in (10cm) will give me excellent warp collapse when using the two yarns as alternate warp stripes.

Tracking

Sometimes after a woven fabric has been washed it will appear to have ridges and furrows over it, sometimes in quite a regular formation. This effect is known as tracking, sometimes called crows' feet. It has been considered a fault and many beginner weavers – and sometimes experienced ones as well – are puzzled by it because the original structure was simply plain weave. It is really just a form of collapse weave caused by unbalanced yarns moving from the straight lines laid down by the original warp and weft threads. For this to happen, as with other collapse weaves, there must be room for the yarns

Active and Passive Yarns

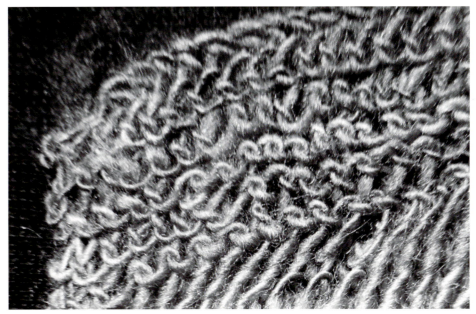

Photo 3-3. Tracking in knitting. Sample knitted by Tracey White.

to move, so it will not happen in a very tightly woven fabric. Tracking is clearer with worsted yarns, and where the yarns have opposing twist directions.

Tracking can also happen in knitting and is caused by the same factors that apply to weaving. When this happens the knitted fabric will pull into diagonal lines and this effect is being used to good effect by some knitting designers.

Warp and weft sett

The number of ends and picks per inch should be less than for a balanced weave. For example, if I use 56/2 yarn for a balanced, plain weave fabric sett at 32 epi, I would weave with approximately 32 ppi. For a collapse weave my usual estimate is two-thirds that of the normal sett, so in this case I would sett and weave with 24 ppi. The warp and weft need to be loose enough to allow the yarns to move while washing.

Because I want movement within the fabric to happen, a 2/2 twill will give more movement than plain weave. Plain weave has a more pronounced pleating effect in the thicker warp stripes.

Collapse Weave

SAMPLE B

This sample, which is an inch or two wider than Sample A, is woven in plain weave, again with the 56/2 (O) as the weft. The 110/2 (S) stripe will pull in more than the thinner 56/2 stripe. This is because the 56/2 warp stripes, after washing, form a balanced weave and the 110/2 stripe is more warp dominant. This effect gives a strong contrast between the two different warp stripes.

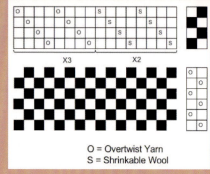

Draft B. Four-shaft

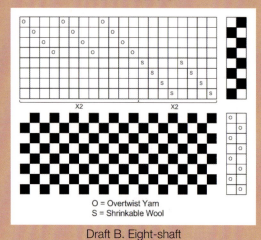

Draft B. Eight-shaft

Active and Passive Yarns

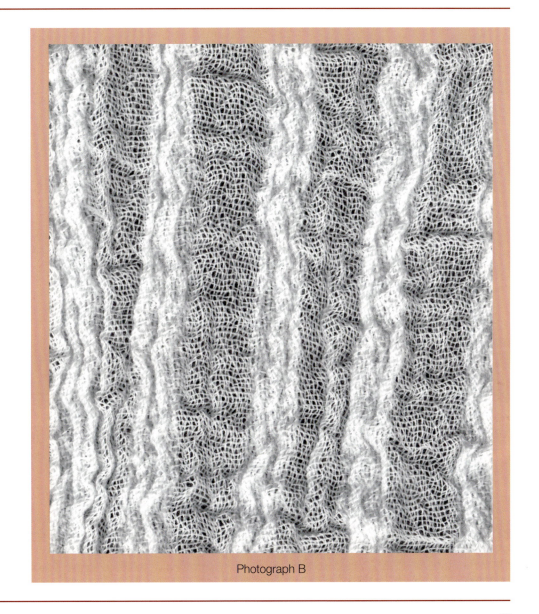

Photograph B

Collapse Weave

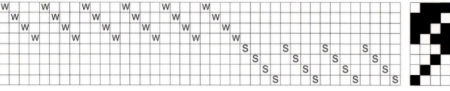

S = Silk

W = Wool

Figure 3-1. Draft for silk and wool fabric.

Worms

If the weft yarn is very highly twisted, it will pull in considerably when washed, sometimes to one third of its original width. This twisted weft has to go somewhere because the width is so drastically reduced. With wool weft yarns, the twist seems to catch in the warp yarns; causing the stripes to buckle and pleat. With silk warp stripes, I have noticed the over-twisted weft can pop up in little curls or worms, as in Photo 3-4. These curls can also pop out at the selvedges after washing, but this can be prevented by setting the selvedge warp ends closer than the rest of the warp, and not leaving loose weft loops at the selvedge. Photo 9-3a shows another example.

The fabric in Photo 3-4 has one-inch stripes of silk and wool alternately in the warp, the 20/2 silk sett at 16 epi and the 56/2 wool sett at 24 epi on an eight-shaft loom. The weft was woven in a 1/3, 3/1 twill with the 56/2 wool as the weft.

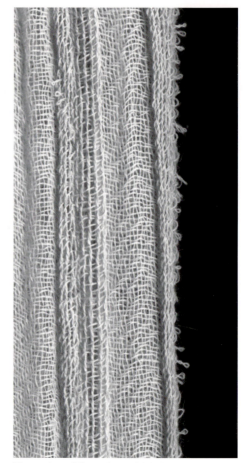

Photo 3-4. Silk and wool fabric.

SAMPLE C

This sample on eight shafts is woven with 3in (8cm) of plain weave, woven in the 56/2 (O) wool. Then an elastic yarn, Lycra (E), is woven for 12 picks. If the elastic yarn is woven as plain weave or twill in these sections, there is not enough pull-in to form waves or pleats. However, if the elastic weft yarn is woven with floats, the pull-in is sufficient to form a collapse cloth. In this sample the elastic weft floats are on Shafts 5-8 (C1) and plain weave is woven on Shafts 1-4, allowing the weft to float over the 56/2 ends on Shafts 5-8. With four shafts, weave as in Draft B but leave a gap of one inch every three inches (7.5cm) in the weft (Photo C).

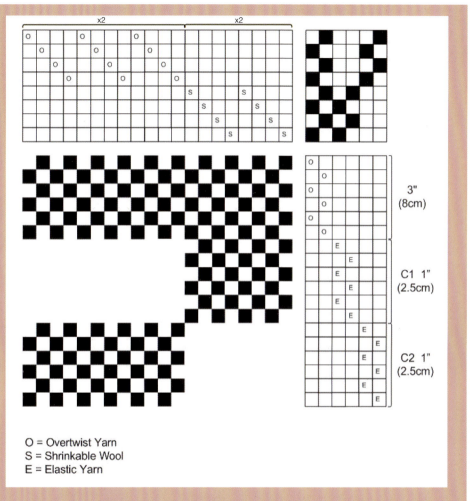

O = Overtwist Yarn
S = Shrinkable Wool
E = Elastic Yarn

Draft C. Eight-shaft

Collapse Weave

Variation for eight shafts
The floats could also be woven on Shafts 1-4 (C2). Alternating between Shafts 1-4 and Shafts 5-8, without plain weave in between, is shown in the photographed Sample C3. See pages 124-126 for more samples with floats.

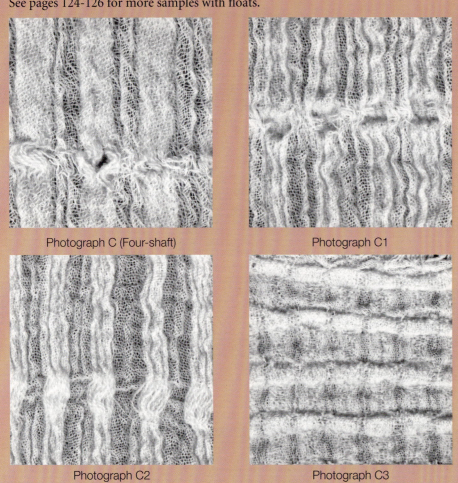

Photograph C (Four-shaft)

Photograph C1

Photograph C2

Photograph C3

Active and Passive Yarns

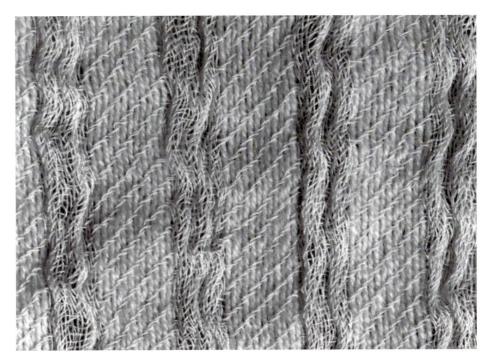

Photo 3-5. Collapse weave fabric in wool with 180/2 in one stripe and 56/2 in the other.

Elastic yarns

Elastic yarns are very useful when weaving collapse weave and are of varying types. Some are smooth until they are washed, others are elastic to begin with. Lycra is a trademark name for the most common elastomeric yarn. These yarns will pull weaving in and are a guaranteed method of weaving collapse fabrics when used as stripes in the weft, or as the complete weft. Some elastic yarns are harsh and cannot be worn next to the skin and sampling is advised.

When weaving with elastic weft yarns, make sure the weft is taut but not stretched. If it is left to lie too loosely it will form loops as in Photo 3-4.

The main difference between elastic yarns and over-twisted yarns is that when the over-twisted yarns relax with washing and the release of tension, they kink and curl. When elastic yarns are washed and the tension is released they contract with no kinks and curls.

Collapse Weave

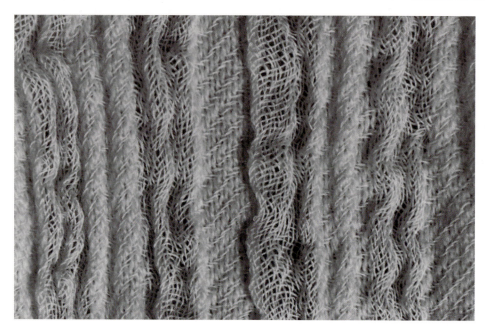

Photo 3-6. Collapse weave fabric in wool with 110/2 in one stripe and 56/2 in the other.

Yarn size

Fine yarns are more flexible than thicker yarns, therefore they will move into pleats and puckers more easily than coarser yarns. If the active yarn is fine and the passive yarn is thick, the collapse will occur only in the fine areas because the thicker yarn is less flexible.

Compare the sample in Photo 3-5 with the sample in Photo 3-6. The thicker warp yarn (180/2 wool) in Photo 3-5 is threaded for one inch at 16 epi with the thinner (56/2 over-twisted wool) threaded for one inch at 24 epi. In Photo 3-6 the thicker warp has been replaced by a finer thread (110/2 wool) and the collapse is more evident. Both these samples were woven in 2/2 twill, with the 56/2 over-twisted wool as the weft (see Draft A). The pick count was 16 to the inch.

PASSIVE YARNS

Passive yarns are those with a balanced twist or little elasticity. Linen, for example, is a

Active and Passive Yarns

Photo 3-7a. Silk and wool collapse.

passive yarn. It does not change with washing and even under tension on the loom it will not stretch. If alternating bands of active and passive yarns are warped, the active yarns will move and pucker and the passive yarns will react according to their strength. If the passive yarns are thicker and stronger, or sett closer, they will retain their flat and stable surface. If they are fine and light, or sett wider apart, they will buckle and curve slightly under pressure from the active yarns.

Silk is more passive than wool because it shrinks less. I have woven with an over-twisted silk as a weft, but found the handle too harsh to wear next to the skin. Washing will not soften this yarn. The silk used in Photo 3-7a is a relatively passive soft silk yarn (20/2) and the 110/2 wool warp stripe has shrunk slightly more than the silk, pulling up the silk stripes. The over-twisted 56/2 wool weft has pulled in the silk more than the wool because the silk stripes retain the open sett allowing movement.

It is helpful to analyze the reasons why yarns behave as they do when weaving samples of collapse weave. In this way we can begin to predict what will happen, although the

Collapse Weave

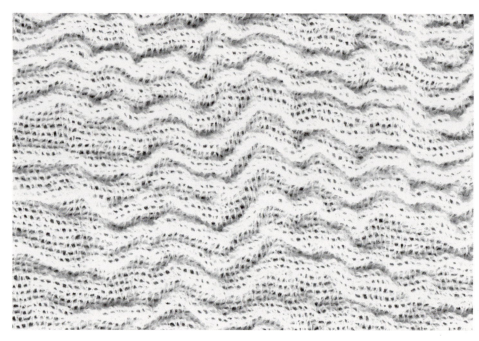

Photo 3-7b. Warp collapse

many surprises make weaving interesting. And collapse weave has more than its share of unexpected happenings. Again, the spacing is important. The sett, the number of threads to one inch (cm), should allow the yarns to move into puckers, but not enough to allow the twist to escape altogether. This can happen at the fringe end, or if the weaving is too loose.

USING ACTIVE AND PASSIVE YARNS
Warp collapse

There are two ways of achieving warp collapse.

In the first case warp collapse happens when the warp ends are of two or more different types with each stripe under different tensions and of varying elasticity, as in Photo 3-7a. Each yarn will pull up at different rates after the release of tension and/or washing, causing the other yarns to form puckers, usually in vertical waves. With collapse weave you can forget about the old adage of not mixing yarn types in the warp.

Active and Passive Yarns

Wrap. 'When I Grow Old I Shall Wear Purple'. Woven by Fran Regan, Australia. Wool, singles and plied, boucle and mohair, dyed with fiber reactive dyes. Photograph Barry Regan

Many different yarns can be used and the wider the variety, the more interesting is the surface texture. The bigger the difference between them, the more collapse. But use these yarns with several of the same type together for maximum effect. A warp with one end of shrinkable wool, one end of mercerized cotton, one end of rayon and one end of bouclé across the width will have little collapse as the different tensions and elasticity are evened out by the close proximity of the different yarns. But warp with half an inch (1cm) of each of these yarns, and the different tensions and pull they exert on each other is magnified and the warp collapse will be strong.

Fine warp yarns will collapse more readily than thicker yarns. In Photo 1-4 there is only warp collapse, caused by the very active wool bouclé used every half inch (1cm) in the warp. If those warp yarns were thicker, the bouclé warp ends would also need to be relatively stronger and more active to achieve the same result.

For most of the finished articles woven in collapse weave, fabric that pleats or waves lengthwise in the cloth gives a better drape when worn. For example, a scarf sits better on the body when the pleats are parallel to the selvedges. Therefore warp collapse is more commonly used, as described above.

In the second method, warp collapse can also cover the entire length of the cloth, as in Photo 3-7b. Use an over-twisted warp yarn, such as the 56/2 wool used in many of my samples, sett at 24 epi, and a stable, soft yarn such as the 110/2 wool yarn as the weft. The weft is beaten loosely at 10-11 picks to the inch, in a plain weave. When the cloth is washed, horizontal pleats will form across the width of the fabric. This will shorten the length considerably, up to 50 per cent after washing if the warp is highly twisted. This type of warp collapse drapes very differently from the collapse described above, and produces a cloth that has lots of bounce.

Weft collapse

Weft collapse happens when the weft is woven with a high-twist or elastic yarn. With washing, these yarns pull the weaving in, the amount depending on the amount of twist in the yarn. This type of collapse causes vertical pleats and waves.

Again, as with warp collapse, finer yarns collapse more readily. If the warp or weft yarns are thicker, more over-twist is necessary.

Both types of collapse can happen in the same fabric, making for some very interesting effects, as can be seen in the sample woven by Sue Foulkes (Photo 3-8). This is an interesting sample in that two different types of over-twisted wool are used in the warp:

Collapse Weave

a black 50/2 crepe which has the highest amount of twist, and an over-twisted, white 56/2 merino. The weft used three yarns: the black crepe, the white 56/2 merino, and a white 1/26 soft single wool yarn, which was not over twisted. The 1/26 was a passive yarn, producing strong collapse because the other high twist yarns distorted it.

The squares were all 3in (7.5cm) square on the loom and were woven with 20 ends per inch and 20 picks per inch (eight per cm) in plain weave. The effect of the very elastic black yarn, which had the strongest influence, is noticeable.

1. The black squares (A), where the black is both warp and weft, are pulled up in both horizontal and vertical directions.
2. The squares (B) at the lower and upper ends of the all black squares are pulled into vertical lines, with the effect seen as stronger with the merino weft (B2). B1, the 1/26 weft spirals slightly.
3. C1, the merino warp, and the 1/26 weft, has a definite spiral pattern, where the horizontal and vertical pleats seem to battle each other.
4. C2, where both the warp and weft are the 56/2 merino, has a more open and indistinct pattern.
5. The squares (D), which have a black weft and a merino warp to the left and right of the all black squares (A), are pulled up into weak horizontal waves.

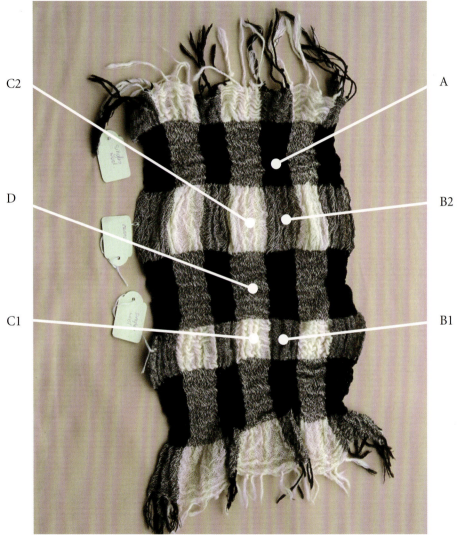

Photo 3-8. Sample woven by Sue Foulkes

Active and Passive Yarns

Scarf *(right)*.
Woven by Sue Foulkes, UK. Warp Collapse.
Warp: over-twisted merino; weft: navy 2/40 botany lambswool and pale blue 2/44NM botany lambswool/silk mix yarn. Double weave, joined in the centre lengthwise. Photographer Martin Foulkes.

Baby Doll dress *(far right)*.
Woven by Anne Field, New Zealand. Over-twisted 56/2 merino wool, acrylic and 110/2 shrinkable merino wool. Dyed with fiber reactive dyes. Designer Anne Field and Sylvia Campbell. Photographer Edward Field.

The black crepe has caused more contraction in the width, the weft, rather than the length. The single 1/26 wool is the most flexible yarn, and has contracted the most in both directions. The 56/2 merino is the least flexible. It can be seen how the pull in each square affects the adjacent squares.

You can see what fun you can have with different types of yarn. Learning how to gauge the different effects of various types of yarns is not always easy, and I cannot stress enough the importance of sampling. I have to admit that I am the type of weaver who finds sampling tedious. My usual method is to wind on a long warp, weave a scarf length, then cut it off the loom, wash it and judge from that whether to continue with that sett, pick count, or weft yarn, the only components I can change at that stage. The problem with

Collapse Weave

Dress, with wrap.
Woven by Anne Field, New Zealand.
Over-twisted 56/2 merino wool, 110/2 shrinkable merino wool.
Designer Sylvia Campbell and Anne Field.
Photographer Edward Field.

Active and Passive Yarns

Photo 3-9. Testing yarn over steam

with this method is that if the finished fabric is not what I want, and changing the sett, pick, or weft yarn will not help, I am left with a wasted warp. So again I suggest you weave the samples and wash them to test your yarn. Make sure you weave samples at least 12in (30cm) long, because the collapse will not happen with shorter samples.

Before the advent of collapse weave, weavers knew that to mix linen and wool together in stripes in either the warp or weft, or both, was to create problems. It was possible to weave with a linen warp and a wool weft, as in linsey-woolsey, without problems but to mix them in the warp created a puckered cloth.

One of my students wove tartan tablemats unknowingly using a mixture of acrylic and wool yarns. When the mat puckered after the first wash, she washed and pressed it several times, hoping to flatten it. What did happen, of course, was that each wash and press caused the wool stripes to shrink and pull the acrylic yarns into even more puckers. She was weaving a collapse weave without knowing it, as the wool yarns shrank and the acrylic did not.

Photo 3-10. Fabric before and after washing

41

Collapse Weave

TESTING YARNS

Determining the properties of the yarns we use is particularly important for collapse weavers. We buy many yarns on cones that have been reused and the information on the cones may be incorrect. A test for wool is that it will burn only in the flame, leaving an ash. Synthetic yarns burn both in and out of the flame and leave a hard bead as a residue.

To test whether a yarn is active or passive, the very high temperature of steam will release the stored energy of over-twisted yarns. If the yarn kinks and curls as the energy is released, it is an active yarn. Hold a loose loop of the yarn over a steaming kettle, and judge the amount it twists around itself. The more it twists back on itself, the more active it is. Because many of the yarns I use are very fine, it is almost impossible to count the number of twists or calculate the twist angle, even with a magnifying glass. If I know the Tex number (as described on page 22) and use the steaming method to estimate the amount of twist, I can make reasonably accurate predictions of how much collapse will happen.

Photo 3-11. Dyed with an airbrush after washing.

FINISHING TECHNIQUES
Fringe finishes
Do the fringe finishes before washing (or keep them very short) because washing will tangle them. Another thing to consider is that when you are using different warp yarns, the fringe may be uneven in length and look untidy. To finish off the fringe ends of collapse weave fabrics for a scarf I usually twist the ends together because this helps the fabric to collapse. A fringe twister is a great help with this. To twist the ends, take two groups of warp ends, twist them firmly in the same direction as they are in their original state, then twist them back together in the opposite direction. The differing shrinkage and take-up rates of the warp yarns in the twisted fringe can vary in length, but I leave this variation because it emphasizes the different yarns. Hemming or hem stitching is not advised because this will straighten out the fabric ends and prevent the collapse.

To make a ripple edge, as in the garment on page 40, straighten out the fabric as it is over-sewn on the sewing machine. A zig zag stitch is ideal for this, but make sure the sewing is very firm by repeating the stitching several times, because this is such an open weave structure. The effect of this 'frou-frou' at the end of collapse weave articles can be very effective.

Washing
All collapse weave fabrics change dramatically when they are taken off the loom and washed. Very active yarns will start collapsing as soon as they are cut from the loom and the tension released, but washing is necessary to allow the collapse to happen to its final stage and to set it.

I use the delicate cycle of my washing machine, making sure I have plenty of water so the fabric can move freely. This cycle uses warm water, gentle agitation with several pauses in the cycle, and a light spin. You will need to experiment with your washing machine to see which is the correct setting. Most of our machines in New Zealand are top loading and this makes it easier, because you can stop the machine to check progress. Lots of water and a very light load make for more agitation than a full load and less water, so take this into consideration too.

If a washing machine is not available, use warm water and agitate the fabric with your fingers until it collapses. This method does give you more control over the process although it takes longer.

Collapse Weave

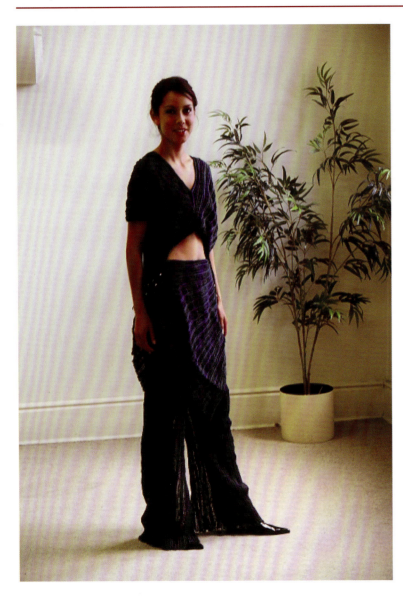

Three-piece outfit of beaded mobius top, pants and over-skirt. 'Nearly Midnight'. Woven by Anne Field, New Zealand. Over-twisted 56/2 merino wool, 110/2 shrinkable merino wool. Dyed with fiber reactive dyes.
Designer Sylvia Campbell and Anne Field.
Photographer Edward Field.

Dry lying flat on a towel. Pulling the fabric lengthwise can help the collapse for weft collapse.

Dyeing

When I first began experimenting with collapse weaves most of the over-twisted yarns were white so dyeing was the only way to achieve color. Now the range of yarns is increasing because of the popularity of this technique, colors are more readily available. Because the yarn must remain over-twisted throughout the weaving process, it can only be dyed in the finishing stages when the weaving is off the loom and after it is washed. I have dyed the complete article, using suitable dyes for the fiber, whether it is cotton, silk, wool or synthetic. Interesting effects are obtained when different types of yarns, or yarns with varying twist counts, take up the dye in different strengths. I have also experimented with spraying dyes onto the finished work. The best results have come from using a spray attachment fired by a compressed air can. This is similar to the air brush technique used by painters. With this attachment I get a very fine spray, which can cover the raised section of the pleats only or just part of the fabric surface. Embroiderers use a dye kit that they blow through to spray dye onto fabric. I have always worried that I would suck instead of blow with these contraptions.

SUMMARY

Characteristics of active yarns:
- They are fine.
- They shrink easily.
- They have an unbalanced twist.
- They are sett and woven with a more open weave than usual.
- They are elastic yarns such as Lycra.

Passive yarns, such as nylon, acrylics, linen, rayon and pre-shrunk wool, have the following qualities:
- They do not change with the release of tension on the loom or with washing.
- They have a balanced twist.
- They have little or no elasticity.
- They are sett and woven at their normal spacing.
- They can be thicker than active yarns.

4 Weave Structure

Weavers know that different weave structures allow a variety of surface textures in cloth. An overshot weave, that is a plain weave background with added pattern weft picks which float over more than one warp end, gives a raised surface to the pattern areas. This is because the plain weave goes over and under each alternate warp thread, while the overshot pattern thread floats over and under several warp ends at once. When washed, the areas with the longer pattern floats tend to puff up, as they are not held down by as many warp threads and have more freedom to move. It can be seen that the longer the floats, the more freedom the yarn has to move, and many deflected warp or weft patterns use this to produce interesting surface textures. Waffle weave, with its long floats outlining a square, is a good example of this. The long floats pull in when washed to outline deep cells.

There are many more structures that will collapse when woven with the correct yarns, and Chapter Nine describes some of these. However, the most common weave structure for collapse weave is to weave with stripes of twill with alternating weft and warp floats.

Photo 4-1. Waffle weave cloth

Figure 4-1. Draft for waffle weave

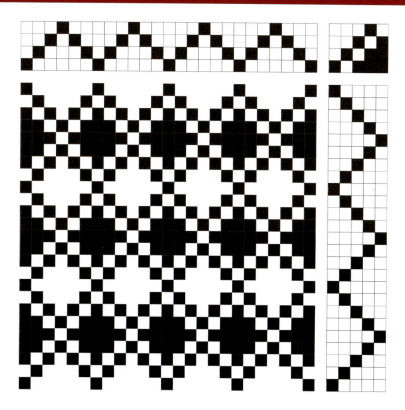

A long float causes more pleating, but too long a float will not be practical because it will snag and the fabric may become unstable.

3/1 AND 1/3 TWILL

A 3/1 twill alternating with stripes of 1/3 twill is the most common structure used in collapse weave. The 3/1 twill stripes are almost warp-face as the weft goes under three and over one warp end. The 1/3 twill stripes are almost weft-face, with the weft going over three warp ends and under one. The warp stripes will puff upwards to form ridges

Collapse Weave

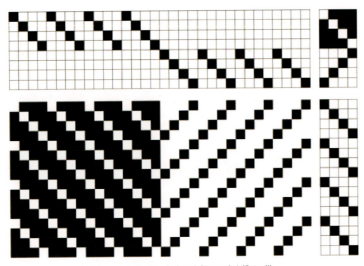

Figure 4-2. Draft for 3/1 and 1/3 twill

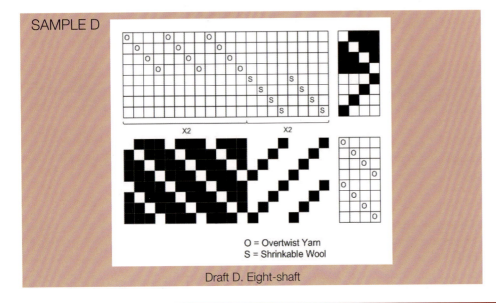

SAMPLE D

O = Overtwist Yarn
S = Shrinkable Wool

Draft D. Eight-shaft

Weave Structure

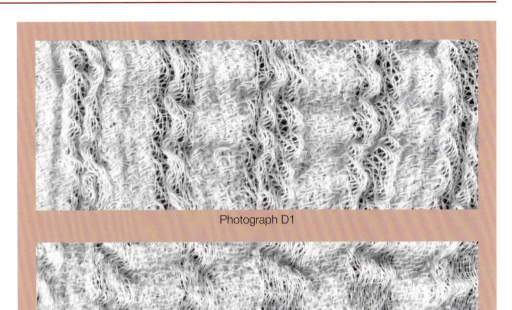

Photograph D1

Photograph D2

This sample can only be woven on an eight-shaft loom. The ridges and hollows are more pronounced because the 1/3 stripes were almost weft-face and the 3/1 stripes were almost warp-face. This sample (1), woven with two types of warp yarn and the over-twist yarn as the weft, is an interesting combination of yarn and weave structure. The over-twist weft yarn gave a softer, less formal surface than those used in photographs 4-2a-f.

Sample 2 has a wool/Lycra blend as the weft.

Collapse Weave

and the weft stripes will recede to form valleys. These pleats are more even and straighter than the wriggly and uneven waves of the collapse weave stripes caused by the yarns discussed in the previous chapter. An eight or more shaft loom is necessary for these weave structures. Follow Figure 4-2 for the threading and weaving.

Width of the stripes
This is a crucial factor. If the stripes are too wide the pleats will flatten out; too narrow and the opposing weft and warp-faced stripes will not have enough room to move.

Sett
This is also an important factor. To weave alternate stripes in 3/1 and 1/3 twill that will collapse you need a sett that is closer than that for plain weave. Too wide or too close a sett and nothing happens. A yarn that I would sett at 16 epi for plain weave, I would sett at 20-24 epi for collapse weave.

Yarn size and type
The pleating is helped if the weft is much finer than the warp yarn, with the weft yarn up to eight times thinner, and woven with more picks per inch than the warp sett. This increases both the density of the fabric and the pleating effect. It can also make the fabric less flexible and slow to weave, as can be seen in Photos 4-2c and 4-2e. Wool weft yarns that shrink during washing pleat better than passive yarns. A better solution may be to use an over-twisted weft as in Photos 4-2g and 4-2h, and in Sample D. Photographs show the surface of the weave but not the handle, so I will indicate the flexibility of the cloth in the accompanying captions. Of course, the flexibility required depends on the end use of the fabric. A scarf needs to be very flexible, a vest less so.

Experiment
You can see where all this is leading. The only way is to experiment. Each time I use a yarn that I have not used before for this type of collapse weave, I have to be prepared to re-sley the reed until I get it right. And this involves weaving a sample that is at least 12in (30cm) long, cutting it off the loom, washing it, then seeing if the amount of collapse is what is required. When I have got the degree of pleating I am aiming for, I keep clear records of the yarn, the sett and the pleat size.

    The warp for all the following samples was 110/2 worsted wool in two contrasting colors. The weft yarns are also wool.

Weave Structure

Photo 4-2a. Weft: same as warp. Sett at 12 epi, 12 ppi, 3/1 and 1/3 twill, 8 ends per stripe, no collapse, flexible

Photo 4-2b. Weft: same as warp. Sett at 16 epi, 16 ppi, 3/1 and 1/3 twill, 8 ends per stripe, some collapse, some flexibility

Photo 4-2c. Weft: 56/2 (thinner than warp). Sett at 16 epi, 16 ppi, 3/1 and 1/3 twill, 16 ends per stripe, some collapse but uneven pleating, flexible

Photo 4-2d. Weft: same as warp. Sett 20 epi, 20 ppi, 16 ends per stripe, 3/1 and 1/3 twill, some collapse, some flexibility

Photo 4-2e. Weft: 56/2 (thinner than warp). Sett 20 epi, 50 ppi, 16 ends per stripe, 3/1 and 1/3 twill, strong collapse, inflexible

Photo 4-2f. Weft: same as warp. Sett 20 epi, 30 ppi, 16 ends per stripe, 3/1 and 1/3 twill, strong collapse, inflexible

Collapse Weave

You can see that the samples with the strongest collapse effect were those with more weft than warp and where the weft was thinner than the warp. The most flexible samples were those using an over-twisted weft. Because this pulled the weaving in, helping the pleating, I did not need to beat so hard, which made the fabric more flexible. Making pleats this way is all a matter of degree. I need to balance the warp and weft size and yarn type, the sett, and the rate of picks per inch (cm).

These samples were all woven with the threading draft shown in Figure 4-2 on an eight-shaft loom.

Color sequence

One effect of these warp and weft-face pleats is that if the collapse is strong enough and the color sequence is as described below, the reverse is a different color to the upper side. In Photos 1-2a and 1-2b the warp stripes were threaded alternately in blue, black, green, black, with a black elastic weft. Therefore, with definite pleats, one side is blue/green and the other side black.

Interesting effects can also be gained by exchanging the weft-face and warp-face areas. These exchange areas can be used to make borders at the end of a scarf, or at random places throughout the fabric length. The color changes can be quite dramatic if the striped warp alternates two

Photo 4-2g. Weft: 56/2 (over-twisted and thinner than warp). Sett 16 epi, 18 ppi, 3/1 and 1/3 twill, some collapse, flexible

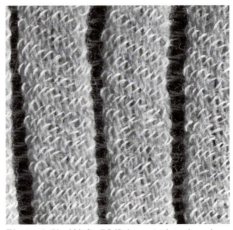

Photo 4-2h. Weft: 56/2 (over-twisted and thinner than warp). Sett 16 epi, 32 ppi (22.5cm), 16 ends per stripe, 3/1 and 1/3 twill, strong collapse, flexible

Photo 4–3. Reversing the pleats

colors, because as the pleats reverse so do the colors. This effect will only be apparent where the collapse is strong enough to overcome the change from warp to weft collapse. If the changes are too close together, or the collapse is weak, the fabric will not be able to reverse. Follow the draft in Figure 4-3 to reverse the pleats.

Collapse Weave

Figure 4-3. Draft for reversing the pleats

Weave Structure

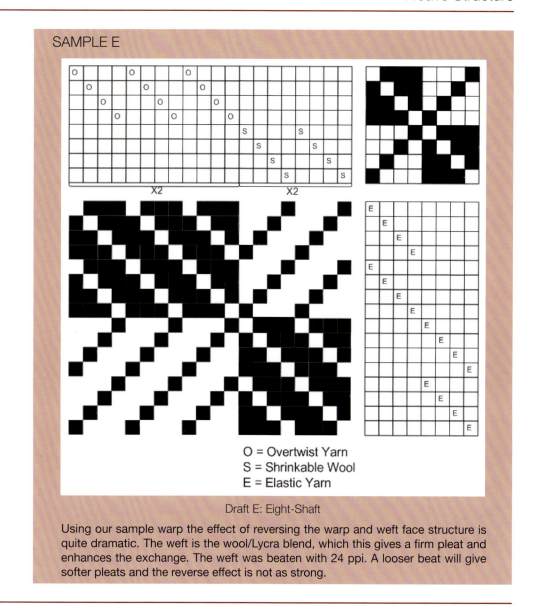

O = Overtwist Yarn
S = Shrinkable Wool
E = Elastic Yarn

Draft E: Eight-Shaft

Using our sample warp the effect of reversing the warp and weft face structure is quite dramatic. The weft is the wool/Lycra blend, which this gives a firm pleat and enhances the exchange. The weft was beaten with 24 ppi. A looser beat will give softer pleats and the reverse effect is not as strong.

Collapse Weave

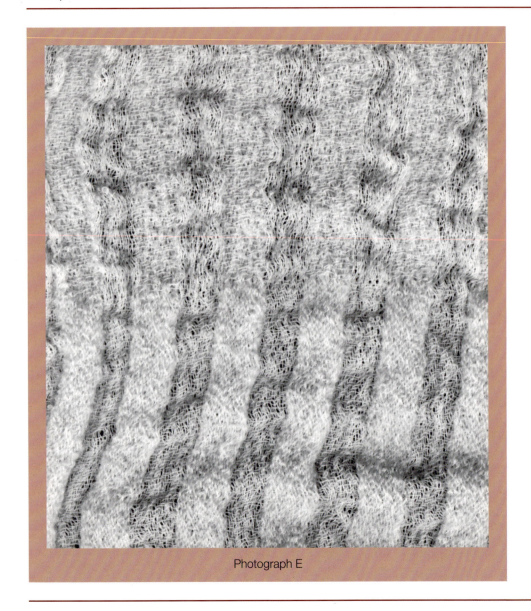

Photograph E

Weave Structure

Contrast areas

Pleats do not have to cover the entire fabric. Many times it is the contrast between different textures that make an interesting surface. I have been experimenting with pleating only the center portion of a wrap, the part that goes around the neck, or the ends of a wrap. The meeting place of the flat with the pleated portion gives an extra dimension to the fabric.

In Photo 4-4 the warp was 110/2, as was the weft in the flat sections, woven in plain weave. The pleated areas were woven with a wool/Lycra blend weft in the 3/1, 1/3 eight-shaft twill draft shown in Figure 4-2. This gave tight, firm pleats that narrowed the fabric. This narrowed area can be at the ends of a scarf or wrap, or in the center.

In Photo 4-5, the warp was threaded with inch stripes alternating between 56/2 wool, sett at 24 epi, and 110/2, sett at 16 epi on a four-shaft loom. The flat area was woven with a weft of 110/2 wool in plain weave. The weft in the collapse areas was woven with a 56/2 over-twisted wool weft. The collapse was softer and less structured, causing ripples rather than pleats.

One of the tests to tell whether a weaver is experienced or not, is that when a piece of weaving is held up against the light any unevenly beaten areas show up instantly. When I am judging weaving, this is one of my tests. Flat areas woven in plain weave take more concentration than pleated areas because any slight variation in beating shows up. So the flat areas of the sample shown in Photos 4-4 and 4-5 were woven in one weaving session, because I tried not to stop once I was into the plain weave areas. Of course you can guarantee that this will be the time when the phone rings and you have to leave the loom.

The pleats do not have to be the same width: a narrow pleat can alternate with a wider pleat, though if the difference is too great the pleating effect will be lost. I keep the pleats to a minimum of one-third of an inch (1cm) and a maximum of one inch, (2.5cm).

Collapse Weave

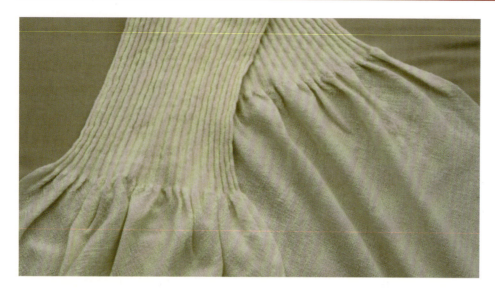

Photo 4-4. Pleating the center area of a wrap.

Photo 4-5. Pleating the ends of a wrap, weaving a 2/2 twill with an over-twisted weft.

Weave Structure

SAMPLE F

O = Overtwist Yarn
S = Shrinkable Wool

Draft F. Four-shaft

O = Overtwist Yarn
S = Shrinkable Wool
E = Elastic Yarn

Draft F. Eight-shaft

Collapse Weave

Four-shaft

The flat area of the fabric is woven as in the treadling in I in plain weave for 6in (15cm) with 110/2 as the weft. Follow this with 6in (15cm) in 56/2 over-twist wool, woven following the twill treadling in II. Short lengths woven in bands such as this will cause the edges in the plain weave areas to bulge out then pull in again in the twill bands. If more than 6 inches is woven in I and II, the effect will be similar to the sample in Photo 4-5. If an elastic weft is used in II instead of the 56/2, the pull in will be more pronounced.

Eight-shaft

In Photo F, the 110/2 wool yarn was threaded all the way across on eight shafts. Bands of treadling I were woven in 110/2 wool with III woven with an all elastic weft, in 3/1, 1/3 twill.

Treadling II is woven with the over-twist wool in a 2/2 twill (not shown).

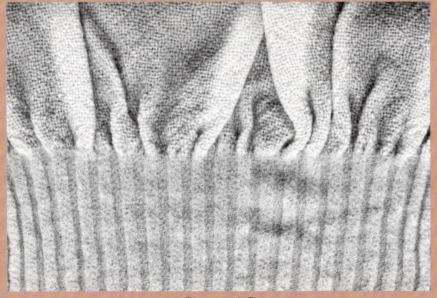

Photograph F

Weave Structure

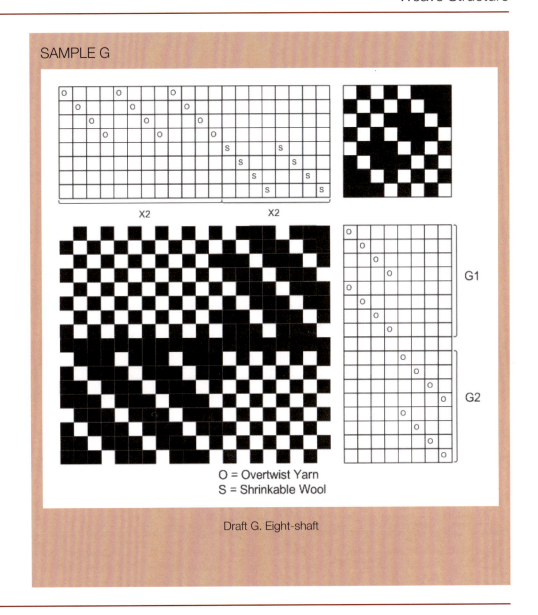

SAMPLE G

O = Overtwist Yarn
S = Shrinkable Wool

Draft G. Eight-shaft

Collapse Weave

In Sample G1, 3/1 twill was woven on Shafts 1-4, which had the 110/2 warp stripes, to give a predominately warp-face stripe. Plain weave was woven on Shafts 5-8, the 56/2 over-twist wool stripe. In Sample G2, Shafts 5-8 were woven with a 3/1 twill to give the warp-face stripe, with Shafts 1-4 woven in plain weave. The weft in both samples was the 56/2 over-twist wool. The two samples had a different surface texture.

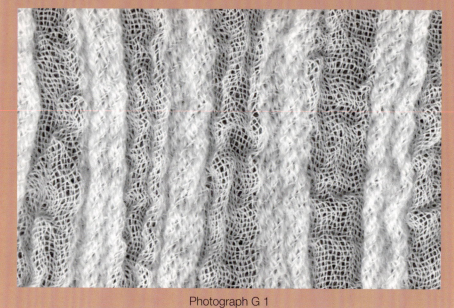

Photograph G 1

Structure changes in stripes

With eight shafts any four-shaft weave can be woven on the first four shafts and another four-shaft weave on the second four shafts. With two different warp yarns, the effect is enhanced. For example, with eight shafts, 3/1 twill can be woven on Shafts 1-4, with plain weave on Shafts 5-8, as in Sample G1. This can be reversed and the difference is apparent (see sample G2). The reason for this is that the two warp yarns, one on Shafts 1-4 and another on Shafts 5-8, are very different. With more shafts the possibilities are even greater.

Weave Structure

Photograph G 2

Collapse Weave

Finishing

The fringes can be finished in various ways. Do not hem because this will flatten the ends and prevent pleating. A twisted fringe should be done before washing and this aids pleating, as described on page 43. Do not weave several picks of plain weave at the beginning and end of the weaving, because this forces the fabric out flat and again will prevent pleating.

Washing the fabric in hot water will assist the pleating effect. While wet, pull the article lengthwise then dry lying flat with the pleats pushed together. If you want to machine wash on a delicate cycle in a washing machine, try a sample first. Too vigorous washing can cause felting.

SUMMARY

Weave structures that aid collapse have:
- Longer floats that will contract when the tension is released or washed.
- Correct width of the stripe to aid the pleating effect.
- Weft yarn much thinner than the warp yarn.
- Over-twisted weft yarn, which causes stronger pleating.

Scarf. Woven and photographed by Sandra Rude, USA. Silk in turned twill with blocks exchanged periodically.

Weave Structure

Wrap. Woven by Anne Field, New Zealand. 110/2 merino wool in plain weave for the centre portion with wool/Lycra™ blend in 3/1 and 1/3 twill for the ends.
Photographer Edward Field

5 Warping and Threading the Loom

Warping the loom when all the warp yarns are the same is not difficult – because the warp yarns are all of one type they will be identical in their behavior. This is the case with the 3/1 and 1/3 twills in Photos 4a-h. However, there are challenges when using two different warp yarns. After a couple of years struggling to put on this type of warp, I finally devised a method that made it a lot easier (then I wondered why I had not thought of it sooner). At the beginning of my collapse weave experiments it rapidly became apparent that winding warps with stripes that were alternately active and passive posed some problems. Some of my warps are 100ft (31m) long and I found that after winding a few yards through the raddle and onto the warp beam, half the warp was two or three feet longer than the other half.

I use a warping mill (a warping board would have the same effect) to wind the warp, and warp from back to front with a raddle, so I will discuss this method first. Later I will cover sectional warping. Two warp beams are a great help, but I will discuss ways around this.

Because the over-twisted warp ends have a tendency to tangle I find winding from back to front is the most satisfactory way. In some of my workshops students have warped from front to back, but even with short warps they took twice as long as the back-to-fronters and the warp seemed to develop a mind of its own as the ends curled around each other.

One solution, even for longer warps, is to wind the warp as described below. When the tension difference between the two warp stripes causes problems, and you are between articles, just cut off the woven length and re-tension and re-tie the warp for the next piece. If you use the lash-on method of tying on, you only waste an inch (2-3cm) or so for the knots.

USING A WARPING MILL OR WARPING BOARD AND RADDLE
Short warps up to 15 feet (4.5m)

Short warps can be wound together, because the difference in stretch and tension between the two types of yarn will not matter. In this case wind the warp as you would normally, changing the yarns as necessary. Using the scarf in Photo 3-6 as an example and Draft A begin with the 110/2 yarn, the thicker wool, and wind one inch sett at 16 epi. Tie on the 56/2, the thinner warp, and wind the next inch sett at 24 epi. Continue winding the warp with alternate stripes in these two yarns, for 21in (54cm), finishing with the 110/2 stripe. A 21in (54cm) width is about as wide as I go because any wider and the collapse disappears in the middle when washed. Start and finish with the thicker, 110/2 warp, because this gives a firmer selvedge.

Because the 56/2 yarn is thin and over-twisted, it has a tendency to tangle and a cross at both ends makes life easier. Put the warp on the warp beam on the loom, put cross sticks through the cross, spread the ends in the raddle at the correct sett (24 e.p.i for the thinner 56/2 yarn, and 16 epi for the thicker yarn). Remove the cross sticks, and wind the warp on under tension through the raddle, with sticks or paper to separate the layers. When you reach the second cross at the other end of the warp, insert the cross sticks through this cross. Thread the ends through the heddles, following the draft in Draft A (page 18). In the reed, space the warp ends with their correct sett. For example, in an eight-dent reed, sley two ends in each dent for the 110/2 ends, and three in each dent for the 56/2 ends.

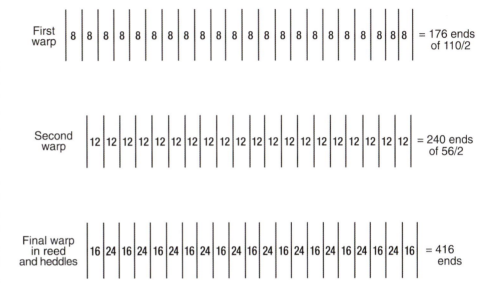

Figure 5-1. Two warps on loom

Collapse Weave

Warps over 15 feet (4.5m) with two warp beams

As with many weaving descriptions, the following explanation sounds more complex when it is written than it is in practice. The illustration in Figure 5-1 should help. The best way is to wind two separate warps, beam them separately onto two warp beams, then thread the heddles with both warps alternately. The two separate warps must be the width of the completed weaving. That is, if the combined warps on the loom will be 21in (54cm) wide, they must be wound onto the loom this width. Again, the scarf in Photo 3-6 and Draft A (page 18) will be used as an example. The thicker, more stable yarn is the 110/2 wool, and this will become the outside two stripes because it gives a secure edge. Wind one warp in the 110/2 yarn. The final sett for this yarn will be 16 epi but as this is only half the warp wind a warp with 22 groups of eight (176 ends). The second warp is the 56/2 wool yarn, which is half the size and has a sett of 24 epi. This warp is wound with 20 groups of 12 ends (240 ends). There are two more groups in the 110/2 yarn because

Photo 5-1. Warp on two beams.

Warping and Threading the Loom

these will be the outside stripes. The stripes in this example are the same size, but this is not necessary – they can vary in width. Both warps have a cross at each end, because the finer yarn tends to tangle easily.

Space the ends of the first warp in the raddle, remove the cross sticks, and wind the warp onto one of the back beams. Place cross sticks in the cross at the other end of the warp, and tie the sticks to the loom structure so they will not interfere with the second warp beam. Wind the second warp onto the other beam in the same manner. The 110/2 warp will be 22in (56cm) wide, and the 56/2 warp will be 20in (51cm) wide. Because they are spaced at half the final sett, they wind smoothly and quickly.

When threading the heddles, take the first group of 16 ends from the outside of the first warp, as they come off the cross sticks, and thread for one inch. Take the first group of 24 ends from the second warp and thread that group for the next inch, and continue across the warp, alternately taking one inch from each group. The first time I did this I was worried that the crossing of the threads would cause tangles, but there were no problems.

Sley the ends in the reed, spacing them according to the correct sett; the finer ends at 24 epi, and the thicker ends at 16 epi. With an eight-dent reed sley the thinner ends at three per dent, and the thicker ends at two per dent. Remove the cross sticks, tie the warp onto the front warp beam, and you are ready to weave.

Collapse Weave

WARPS OVER 15 FEET (4.5M) WITH ONLY ONE WARP BEAM

Wind both warps as on page 68 and 69 and put the first warp on the loom. The second warp can be attached in two ways.

First method

Wind the second warp onto the back beam of a table loom of the correct width, using a raddle and bringing the warp over the back beam as in Figure 5-2. Place the table loom at the back of the main loom, with its back roller and ratchets close to the main loom, but slightly higher. The height difference is to keep the two warps apart. Put the cross sticks in the cross at the end of this second warp. You will need to suspend them from something. If your main loom has some type of upper structure, suspend them from this. It may be possible to hang a smooth wooden rod from the main loom, bring the second warp over this, then through the cross sticks. The cross should be close enough to your heddle threading position so you can reach the cross in both warps at once. Weavers are known for their ingenuity. I have even suspended rods from hooks in the ceiling over my loom. Thread the heddles, sley, and tie on as described earlier. When weaving, you will need to advance both warps separately.

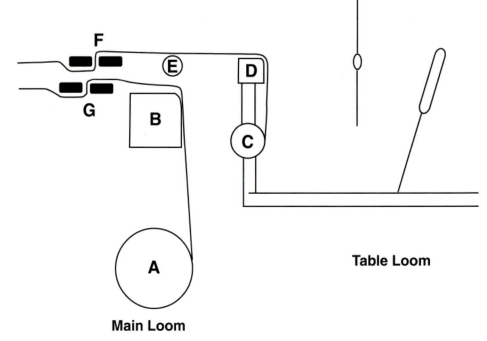

Figure 5-2. Using a table loom as a second beam

A. Warp roller on main loom.
B. Warp beam on main loom.
C. Warp roller on table loom.
D. Warp beam on table loom.
E. Rod suspended from main loom.
F. Cross sticks through warp on table loom.
G. Cross sticks through warp on main loom.

Warping and Threading the Loom

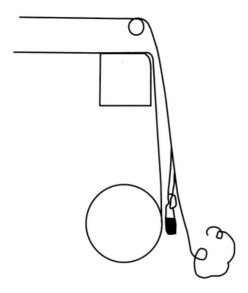

Figure 5-3. Hanging a weight from a second warp

Second method

Wind the second warp as before. Then take it over a rod attached to the back of the loom so it hangs slightly above the first warp on the back beam. Put the cross sticks through the warp cross between the rod and the heddles, and thread the heddles and sley as described earlier. When you are ready to begin weaving tie a cord around this second warp between the floor and suspended rod and attach a weight. A plastic bottle (with a handle) filled with water is excellent for this, because you can add or take away water until the tension is the same on both warps. You do need to move the position of the cord and bottle every time you advance the warp.

SECTIONAL WARPING

At first glance this seems an easier way to warp, because each space on the sectional beam can have its own narrow warp held at a different tension. However, the spacing of the sectional flanges determines the width of each stripe. If the flanges are an inch apart, the scarf warp described in the earlier section of this chapter, which has alternate inch stripes of 110/2 and 56/2 warp is easy. However, if you have flanges 2 inches (5cm) apart, this would have to be the stripe width. The flanges limit the size of the stripes. To get the variety of stripe width, it is probably best to use the sectional beams as plain beams.

6 Four-shaft Double Weave

Adding layers to collapse weave fabric opens many possibilities. The previous chapters have covered one-layer fabrics where some areas collapse and some do not. With more than one layer, as in double weaves, one layer, or part of it, can collapse while another layer does not. Or both layers can collapse. The layers can interchange in both the warp and the weft, or the layers can be joined at intervals with a pick-up technique. One layer can be smooth, the other pleated. There are many possibilities. With four-shaft double weave, two layers can be woven with each layer weaving plain weave (tabby); with eight shafts the two layers can each weave 2/2 twills, or four layers can be woven in plain weave. As you add more shafts on your loom, the layers can become more numerous and the weave structures more complex.

The following photographed samples (6-1 to 6-6) were 15in (38cm) wide on the loom and each layer was woven with 16 picks to the inch. The black areas in most samples show very little definition.

FOUR-SHAFT DOUBLE WEAVE

With four shafts it is possible to weave plain weave on both layers, with one layer on two of the shafts and the other layer on the other two shafts. Plain weave is stable but although it is not as flexible or as soft as twill weaves, a very satisfactory collapse fabric can be woven. In fact with some of the following samples plain weave collapse achieves an attractive rippled surface, while a 2/2 twill has a flatter texture – exactly the opposite to what one would expect. The amount of over-twist in the yarn determines the amount of collapse possible.

Winding the warp

When winding the warp for double weave wind both layers together, unless you have two warp beams for two separate warps. Samples 6-1 to 6-6 have one layer white, the other black. Block A is wound with one white and one black warp end together for one inch, with 16 black and 16 white ends. The black and white yarns are both 110/2 wool. Block B is wound with three white ends (56/2) to two black ends (110/2), with 16 black ends and 24 white ends for one inch. The white warp is divided into alternating stripes, as with the sample in Photo 3-6 and Draft A (page 18), and using the same yarns, allowing a rippled texture when woven and washed. The black layer has just one yarn, 110/2, giving

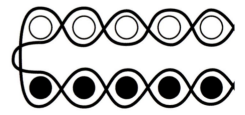

Figure 6-1a. Cross section of four-shaft double weave.

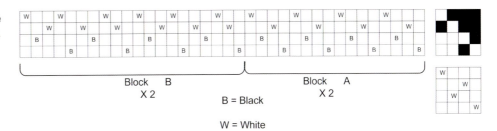

Figure 6-1b. Draft for two-layer tube, single white weft.

a smooth surface when collapsed. This gives a different surface texture to each layer in the finished weaving.

Do not make a very long warp for your first attempt, and follow the advice in Chapter Five.

With two warp beams the black and white warps can be wound and beamed separately. Because double weave has twice the number of ends compared to a single layer, more heddles are used.

The white warp is threaded on Shafts 3 and 4 and the black warp ends are threaded on Shafts 1 and 2. Threading the two layers where the sett for both yarns is the same, as in Block A, is simple. A black end on Shaft 1 is followed by a white end on Shaft 3, then a black on Shaft 2, followed by a white end on Shaft 4, and so on. Repeat Block A twice for 32 ends, 16 black and 16 white. In an eight-dent reed these ends would be sleyed four to a dent.

Block B, where the white ends on Shafts 3 and 4 have three ends to every two black, is threaded differently from Block A, although the white and black are still on the same shafts as in Block A. Block B begins with a black end on Shaft 1, followed by a white end on Shaft 3 and a white end on Shaft 4, then a black end on Shaft 2, followed by a white end on Shaft 3 and so on. In other words, each black end is followed by one white end, then two white ends alternately. The threading took much longer than the actual weaving of these samples, as is the case with much collapse weaving. Block B, with an eight-dent reed, has five ends sleyed in each dent – three white and two black.

Weaving the black and the white layers separately, without joining them at the edges to make a tube or without any interchange between the two layers, makes no sense. It would

Collapse Weave

be easier to weave two separate fabrics, one black and one white, and it would be much quicker too. So the layers have to be connected in some way, and there are various ways of doing this.

In these samples (6-1 to 6-6) the white weft is the 56/2 over-twisted wool and the black weft is either a 1/30 crepe wool or 110/2 wool. The 1/30 is a singles yarn with a very high twist. The white 56/2 is not as highly twisted as the 1/30.

Weaving a tube, method one

Follow the treadling draft in Figure 6-1b. With the white 56/2 weft the first pick weaves in the top layer by lifting Shaft 3. Then Shafts 3 and 4 of the white warp are both lifted up out of the way, along with Shaft 1 of the black warp and the same weft weaves the first pick in the lower layer. Pick three, lifting Shaft 4, weaves the upper layer again, followed by pick four, completing the lower layer. If you have not woven double weave before, it is worth remembering that to weave the lower layer, all the upper layer ends must be lifted out of the way first. Also you cannot see what is happening in the lower layer and this can lead to unpleasant surprises when the warp is cut off. A mirror held underneath the weaving can be reassuring. Beat with 16 ppi.

Both layers in Photos 6-1a and 6-1b collapsed more at the selvedges than

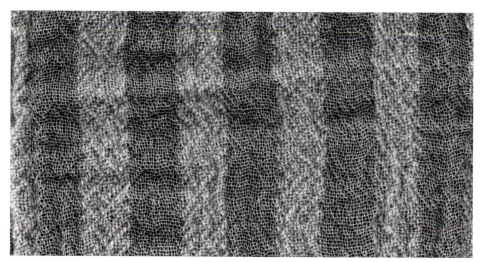

Photo 6-1a. Weaving a tube with a single, white weft. Front.

Photo 6-1b. Weaving a tube with a single, white weft. Back

Four-shaft Double Weave

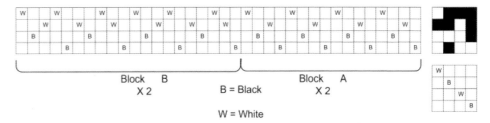

Figure 6-2. Weaving a tube by joining at the selvedges

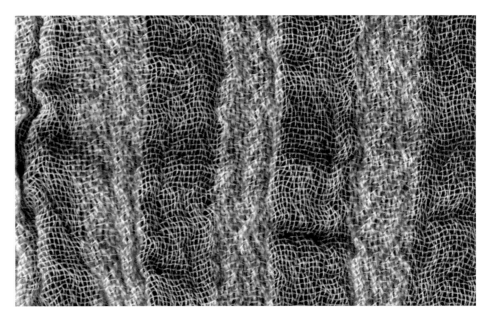

Photo 6-2. Weaving a tube by joining at the selvedges

Collapse Weave

in the center. The center portion of the lower layer, with the black warp and white weft, looks more like tracking than collapse but the texture is interesting in comparison to the top layer. The samples contracted from 15in (38cm) to 10in (25cm) after washing.

Weaving a tube, method two

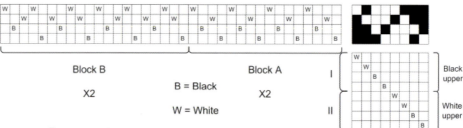

Figure 6-3. Draft for exchanging two layers.

The advantage of this method of weaving a tube is that each layer can be woven with a matching colored weft: black 1/30 for the black warp layer and white 56/2 for the white warp layer. In this way the two layers are striking in their color contrast. Weave a white and black pick alternately, following the treadling instructions in Draft 6-2. Catch the wefts around each other at the selvedge by developing a method where one shuttle goes under or over the other.

The black 1/30 weft certainly pulled in the sample in Photo 6-2 considerably, causing ripples on the black layer and contracting the width from 15in (38 cm) to 8in (20cm). The black 1/30 is finer and has more twist than the white 56/2.

Exchanging two layers

Reading the treadling draft in Figure 6-3, Block I has the black layer up and the white layer down. Block II is the opposite: black is down and white up. For Block I weave the first two picks in the white weft, and third and fourth picks with the black

Photo 6-3. Exchanging two layers

Four-shaft Double Weave

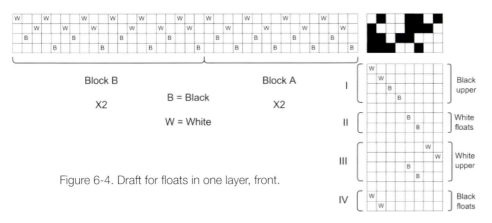

Figure 6-4. Draft for floats in one layer, front.

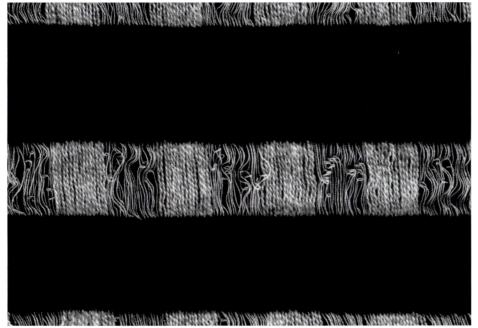

Photo 6-4a. Floats in one layer, front.

weft, taking care not to catch the black and white weft threads around each other at the selvedge. The two layers are separate at this stage. Repeat this as necessary.

To exchange the layers weave Block II; the first two picks with the white weft and the third and fourth picks in the black weft. If the layers are exchanged frequently there will be no collapse. An effective way to use this technique is to weave half a scarf (or any length of fabric) as Block I, then the other half as Block II. The exchange area is shown in Photo 6-3.

Floats

The floats cannot be too long because they will snag. In Photos 6-4a and 6-4b the floats were 1 1/4 inches (3cm) long, and this would be long enough for most wearable articles like a scarf. The interest in this sample comes from the 56/2 warp floats which kink and curl. The photographed sample (6-4a and 6-4b) has warp collapse only because the black layer was woven with the 110/2 yarn, which is not over-twisted. If the black layer had been woven with the 1/30, there would be some collapse. The white layer was woven with 56/2 as the weft, but the effect of the stronger black wool kept the collapse out. Block I has the black warp woven as the top layer, Block II has the black layer woven as the lower layer, leaving the white warp floating, as in the sample. The layers

Collapse Weave

can be exchanged. To weave with the white layer on top, follow Block III, then for the black floats in the upper layer, weave Block IV. The layers must exchange because with both white floats and white weaving in the upper layer, the two layers will not be joined together.

Floats in both layers

For this sample (6-5) the black warp was woven alternately in the upper and lower layers, with the white floats also alternating layers. Block I, with white floats in the lower layer, is followed by Block II, with white floats in the upper layer. In the draft there are 32 weft picks in each block, but this can be varied, and the blocks do not have to be of equal length. Again, keep the floats to a manageable length. To weave black floats, weave Block III followed by Block IV. The back of the fabric is the same as the front.

Photo 6-4b. Floats in one layer, back.

Four-shaft Double Weave

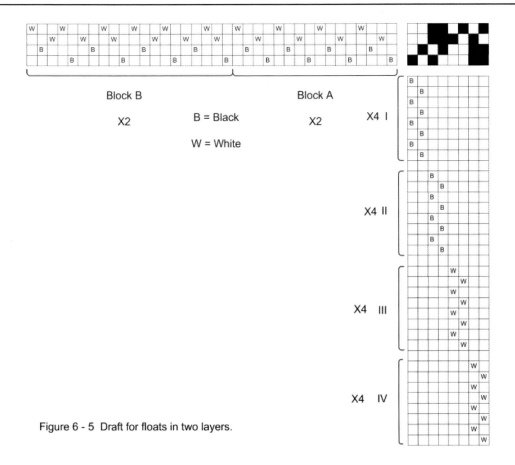

Figure 6 - 5 Draft for floats in two layers.

Collapse Weave

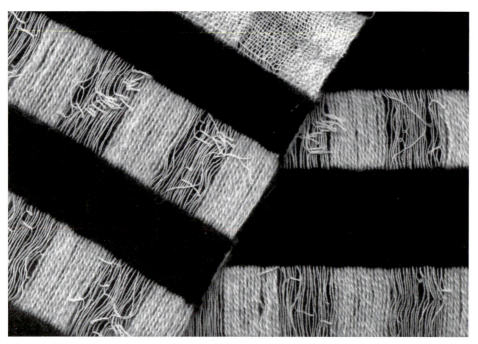

Photo 6-5a. Floats in two layers, front and back.

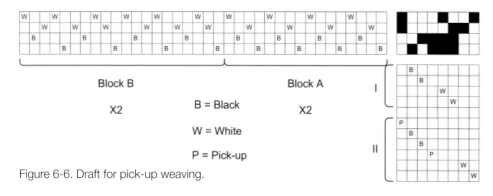

Figure 6-6. Draft for pick-up weaving.

Joining two layers with pick-up weaving

This technique brings part of one layer up through the other, tying down the two layers at intervals. The white weft is the 56/2, the black weft is 1/30. Weave several inches with the black layer upper, as in Block I. To exchange layers begin with the pick in Block II as follows:

1. Lift Shafts 3 and 4, bringing all the white ends to the surface. With a pick-up stick (smooth stick with a pointed end) pick up the sections of the white layer that you want to exchange. Drop Shafts 3 and 4 and push the stick up against the reed.
2. Lift Shaft 1 and throw the shuttle with the black weft through the shed. The pick-up stick holds the ends on the stick above the weft, and they will not be woven. Do not beat.
3. Drop Shaft 1, lift Shaft 2 and return the black weft through the shed. Drop Shaft 2, remove the pick-up stick and beat both picks into place.
4. Lift Shafts 1 and 2, bringing all the black ends to the surface. Pick-up the *background* ends, the ends you do not want to exchange, onto the pick-up stick. Drop Shafts 1 and 2, and push the pick-up stick back against the reed.
5. Lift Shaft 3, and throw the white weft through the shed. This shed will not

Four-shaft Double Weave

be as clear as the shed in Steps 1 and 2, but working the pick-up stick back and forth a few times up and down the warp will help. Do not beat.

6. Drop Shaft 3, lift Shaft 4, and return the white weft back through the shed. Drop Shaft 4, remove the pick-up stick and beat both picks into place.

In the sample (6a and 6b) the exchange areas were woven by repeating Block II twice. The exchange area does not need to be large, because it is just holding the layers together at one point, and this point does not need to be at the same place each exchange.

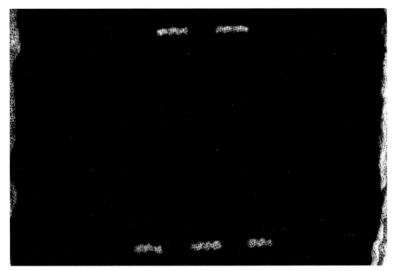
Photo 6-6a. Pick-up weaving, front.

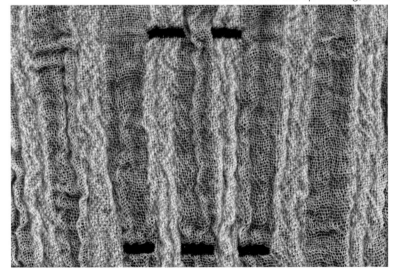
Photo 6-6a. Pick-up weaving, back.

7 Eight- to Sixteen-shaft Double Weave and Supplementary Warps

EIGHT-SHAFT DOUBLE WEAVE

With eight shafts twills can be woven. This usually makes the cloth more flexible than plain weave. The black, plain weave areas are more ribbed than in the twill samples. The yarns in these eight-shaft samples are the ones used for the four-shaft samples in Chapter Six.

2/2 twill/plain weave tube

The draft in Figure 7-1 has the upper white layer weaving a 2/2 twill and the lower black layer weaving plain weave. The white weft (56/2) weaves the first pick in the top layer by lifting Shafts 5 and 6 for the first twill pick. Then Shafts 5, 6, 7, 8, of the white warp are lifted up out of the way, along with Shafts 1 and 3 of the black warp and the same weft continues across the lower layer in plain weave. Pick three, lifting Shafts 6 and 7, weaves the upper layer again, followed by pick four, with Shafts 5, 6, 7, 8, along with Shafts 2 and 4 in the lower layer. And so on as in Figure 7-1. To weave 2/2 twill in both layers weave the draft in Figure 7-2 but with an all white weft.

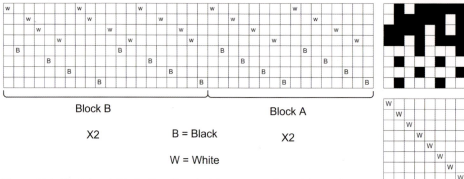

Figure 7-1. Draft for eight shaft twill and plain weave tube, white weft.

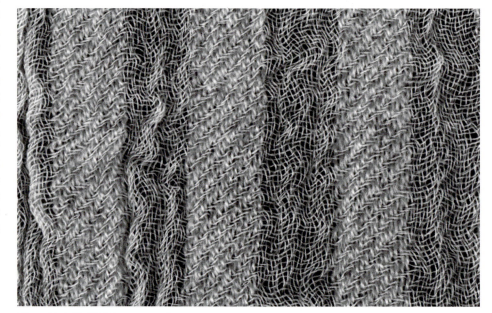

Photo 7-1. Twill/plain weave tube.

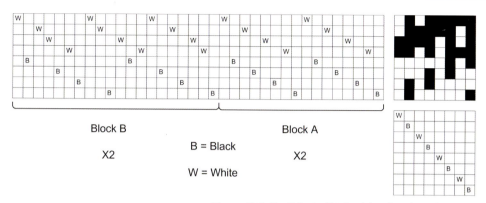

Figure 7-2. Draft for twill tube joined at the selvedges

Weaving a tube in 2/2 twill joined at selvedges

As with Method Two on page 76, the advantage with weaving a tube this way is that both layers use the contrasting weft colors. The white weft is the 56/2, the black weft 1/30. Catch the two weft colors around each other at the selvedges. The sample in Photo 7-2 has been folded to show one selvedge.

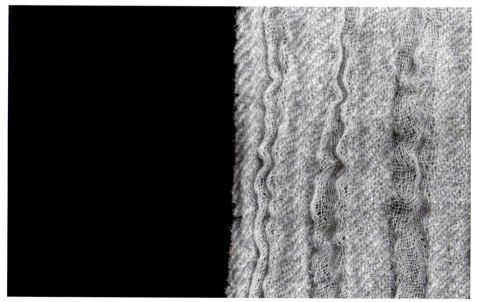

Photo 7-2. 2/2 twill tube joined at the selvedges

Collapse Weave

Weaving a 3/1 twill and plain weave tube joined at the selvedges

With eight shafts you can also weave a 3/1 or 1/3 twill. This sample (7-3) has a 3/1 twill woven in the white upper layer in the 56/2 with a plain weave woven in the black lower layer in the 1/30 weft. The 3/1 twill pulls the width of the woven sample in by 2in (5cm) more than the other eight-shaft samples and the pleats are more pronounced.

Complex eight- and twelve-shaft double weaves

These three samples (7-1 to 7-3) give some indication of the variety of weave structures that can be woven on an eight-shaft loom. These techniques can be combined to exchange layers, weave floats, and pick-up weaves. However, unless you are weaving on a table or dobby loom, to weave many of these techniques with twill weaves in both layers requires many treadles and most eight-shaft floor looms have a limit of 10 treadles.

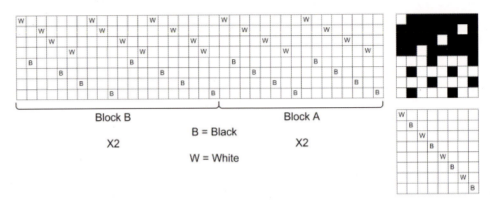

Figure 7-3. Draft for 3/1 twill and plain weave tube joined at the selvedges

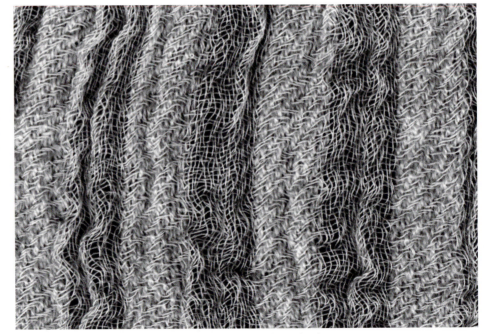

Photo 7-3. 3/1 twill and plain weave tube joined at the selvedges

Eight- to Sixteen-shaft Double Weave and Supplementary Warps

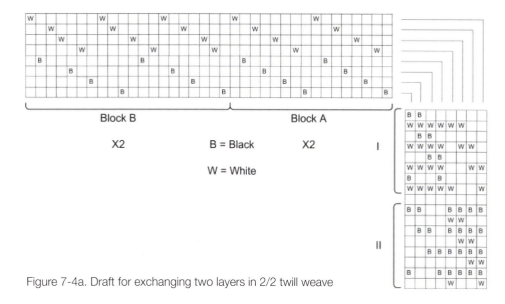

Figure 7-4a. Draft for exchanging two layers in 2/2 twill weave

Exchanging two layers in 2/2 twill (eight shafts)

Exchanging layers with 2/2 twill in both layers would need 16 treadles, as shown in Draft 7-4a, which has been written for an eight-shaft dobby or table loom. The weft colors are shown in the treadling. For example, Pick 1 has a black 1/30 weft weaving on Shafts 1 and 2. The second pick has the first four shafts lifted out of the way, and a white 56/2 weft weaving on Shafts 5 and 6. The colors indicated in the treadling are the color of the weft picks, not the color of the shafts to be lifted. Block I has the black layer uppermost, Block II the white layer up.

Collapse Weave

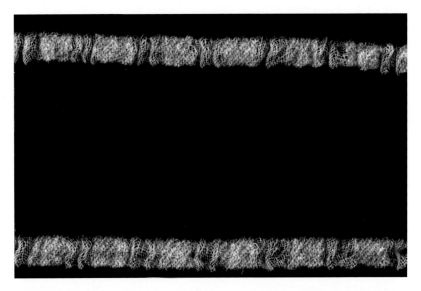

Photo 7-4a. Exchanging two layers in 2/2 twill, front

Photo 7-4b. Exchanging two layers in 2/2 twill, back.

Eight- to Sixteen-shaft Double Weave and Supplementary Warps

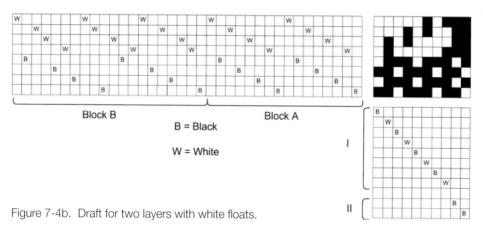

Figure 7-4b. Draft for two layers with white floats.

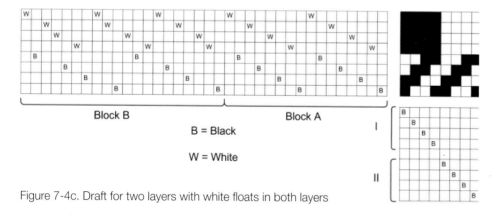

Figure 7-4c. Draft for two layers with white floats in both layers

Two layers with white floats (eight shafts)

There are no photographed samples for Figures 7-4b and 7-4c. In Figure 7-4b Block I, the black layer is woven in plain weave, the white layer woven in 2/2 twill. In Block II, the white warp floats over the black weave, still in plain weave. This requires 10 treadles.

In Figure 7-4c only the black layer is woven. Block I has floats in the upper white layer, and the lower black layer is weaving a 2/2 twill. To change the white floats to the lower layer, Block II is woven with just the black warp uppermost, again weaving in a 2/2 twill weave.

Collapse Weave

Twelve-shaft double weave

With 12 shafts, the combination of layers becomes more complex. In this one sample (Photos 7-5a and 5b) I have included, the pleating effect is very defined with a three dimensional appearance to both sides of the cloth, even although each side is very different. Block A in the threading draft is threaded with 110/2 for both the black and the white warp ends. Block B has the 56/2 as the white warp ends, with three white ends to every two black ends.

Block I. This section was woven with the black upper layer and the white lower layer, both in plain weave for 1 inch. The white weft was 56/2 wool, used in the previous samples. The black weft is 110/2 wool.

Block II. The weft used for the white weft floats in Block II is a Lycra/wool blend, which exerts a strong pull widthways on both layers. The floats cover only part of the white warp, the 56/2 stripes, on Shafts 9 to 12. The thicker 110/2 warp, on Shafts 5-8 is woven in plain weave. Block II was also woven for 1 inch.

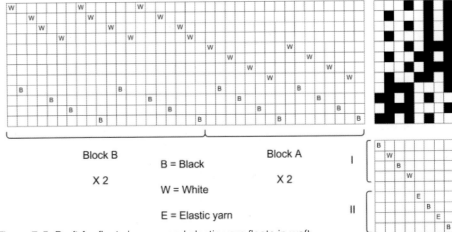

Figure 7-5. Draft for floats in warp and elastic yarn floats in weft

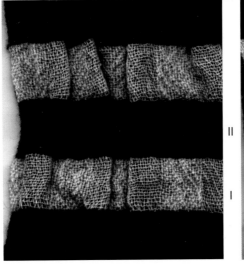

Photo 7-5a. Floats in white elastic/wool blend. Front.

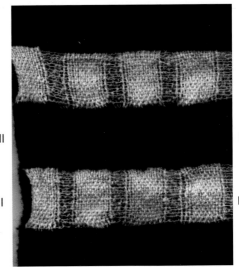

Photo 7-5b. Floats in white elastic/wool blend. Back.

Eight- to Sixteen-shaft Double Weave and Supplementary Warps

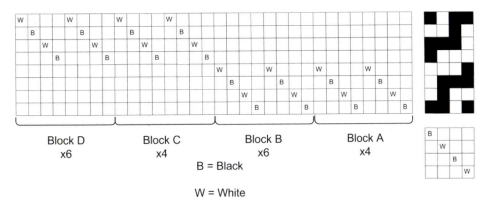

Figure 7-6a. Draft for eight-shaft vertical interchange in plain weave

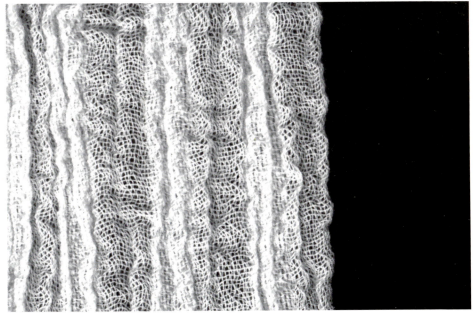

Photo 7-6. Vertical interchange in plain weave

EXCHANGING VERTICAL LAYERS (EIGHT SHAFTS)
Plain weave layers

Eight shafts are necessary for plain weave layers.

Thread Blocks A and B of the threading draft (7-6a) for half the width, with Blocks C and D in the other half. Black ends are on Shafts 1, 3, 5, and 7, white ends are on Shafts 2, 4, 6, and 8. The warp yarns used in the sample are 110/2 in black and white, and 56/2 wool in black and white, with one inch of each. The 110/2 was sett at 32 epi, following Block A and C in the threading draft, and the 56/2 was sett at 48 epi, following Blocks B and D. Repeat the blocks as required, but finish on the A block. When the layers are separated, the sett is 16 epi for the 110/2 and 24 epi for the 56/2 yarn. Winding the warp is much quicker if the two ends can be warped together, taking care to separate them with your fingers.

The weft for the black layer was 1/30 wool, a very highly twisted merino singles which pulled in more than the white 56/2 merino wool. The weft for the white layer was the 56/2. Both layers were woven with 16 ppi. The four picks of the repeat are as follows:

1. The black weft goes over the white warp in Blocks A and B and under in Blocks C and D.

Collapse Weave

2. The white weft goes under the black warp in Blocks A and B and over in Blocks C and D.
3. The black weft goes over the white warp in Blocks A and B and under in Blocks C and D.
4. The white weft goes under the black warp in Blocks A and B and over in Blocks C and D.

Reversing the layers

The layers can be changed horizontally by reversing the layers. Remember to weave a full repeat of each block before weaving the next block. Weave the treadling draft in Figure 7-6a, followed by the draft in Figure 7-6b. There is no photographed sample for this draft.

Separate layers with interchanges

Weave with the draft in Figure 7-6c for the required length and with the black layer uppermost, then weave the treadling in Figure 7-6b. Repeat Figure 7-6c, then follow with the treadling in Figure 7-6a. Interchanging the drafts like this is easier on a table or dobby loom, otherwise you are forever crawling under your loom to re-tie the treadles. Photo 7-7c shows the placement of the blocks.

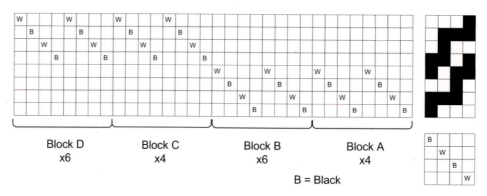

Figure 7-6b. Draft for reversing the layers

B = Black
W = White

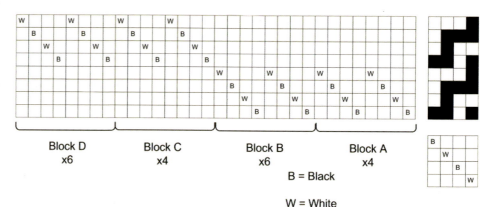

Figure 7-6c. Draft for separate layers with interchanges

B = Black
W = White

Eight- to Sixteen-shaft Double Weave and Supplementary Warps

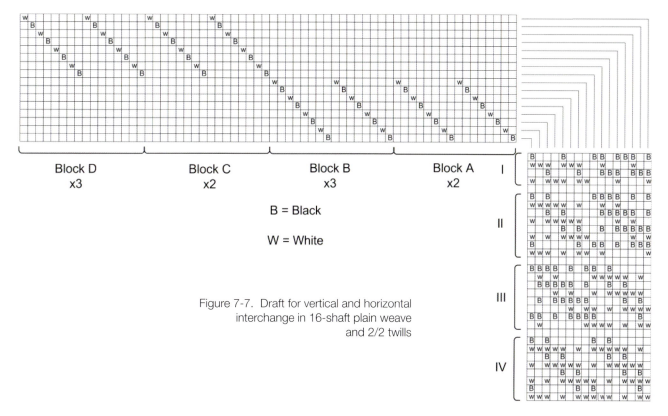

Figure 7-7. Draft for vertical and horizontal interchange in 16-shaft plain weave and 2/2 twills

SIXTEEN-SHAFT TWILL: EXCHANGING THE LAYERS

Weaving a 2/2 twill on 16 shafts makes a softer, more flexible cloth than plain weave. As most 16-shaft floor looms are dobby looms, I will write the drafts for use on these looms. A 16-shaft table loom could also be used. Read the instructions for warping and threading on page 89, because these are the same as those for the eight-shaft drafts. The threading draft uses the same yarns as the eight-shaft drafts in Figures 7-6a to 7-6c on page 89. The colors shown in the treadling draft are the colors of the weft picks, not the colors of the shafts to be lifted. Block I in Figure 7-7 is for plain weave. Blocks II to IV are for twill weaves.

Collapse Weave

Vertical interchange
Block I, Figure 7-7. Plain weave on 16 shafts, with the black layer uppermost in Blocks A and B of the threading draft. The white layer is uppermost in Blocks C and D (see Photo 7-6).

Vertical interchange in 2/2 twill
Block II, Figure 7-7. 2/2 twill, with black layer uppermost in Blocks A and B, and white uppermost in Blocks C and D.

Vertical and horizontal interchange
Block III, Figure 7-7, 2/2 twill with the white uppermost in Blocks A and B and black uppermost in Blocks C and D. To weave with horizontal and vertical interchanges, exchange Blocks II and III at intervals.

Separate layers joined in blocks
Block IV, Figure 7-7. Separate layers with black in the upper layer and white in the lower layer. To join the layers, alternate sections where the layers are separate with Blocks II and III. Lifting 12 shafts at once on a floor loom is very good exercise for the leg muscles!

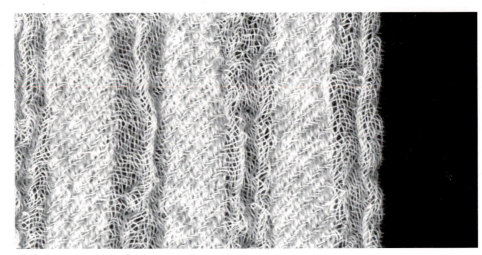
Photo 7-7a. Vertical interchange in 2/2 twill

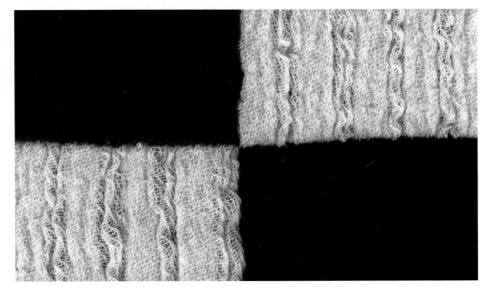
Photo 7-7b. Vertical and horizontal interchange

Eight- to Sixteen-shaft Double Weave and Supplementary Warps

Photo 7-7c. Separate layers joined in blocks

Collapse Weave

SUPPLEMENTARY WARPS

When you are weaving two layers it is not necessary to have both warps the same width. In the following samples a supplementary warp layer has been added above the lower layer. Both layers can collapse, or one layer can be woven flat with the other collapsing. The samples in Photos 7-8 and 7-9 are woven with the same warp and weft yarns as many of the earlier samples in this chapter, described on page 72. Block A in the threading draft Figure 7-8a is the outer single black layer that is threaded as often as desired. Block B has alternate ends of black 110/2 and white 110/2 with each layer sett at 16 epi. Block C has black 110/2, sett at 16 epi on Shafts 1-4 and white 56/2 on Shafts 5-8, the white stripe sett at 24 ep.i. This gives a ribbed effect to the white layer.

Supplementary warp with both layers collapsing

In this sample (Photo 7-8) the supplementary warp is 3in (8cm) wide and placed slightly off-center, with both layers woven with an over-twisted weft, using white 56/2 for the upper layer and black 1/30 for the lower layer. The white supplementary warp is attached to the base by exchanging the two layers for four picks at intervals. Where the layers exchange the supplementary warp is stretched out and

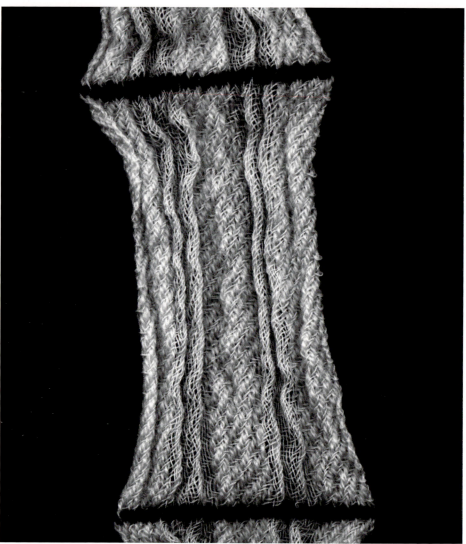

Photo 7-8. Supplementary warp in 2/2 twill joined to lower layer at intervals

Eight- to Sixteen-shaft Double Weave and Supplementary Warps

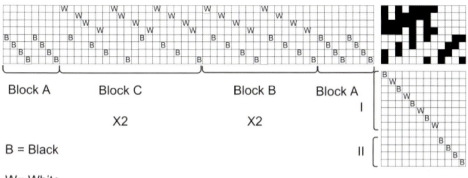

Figure 7-8a. Draft for supplementary warp, 2/2 twill joined to lower layer at intervals

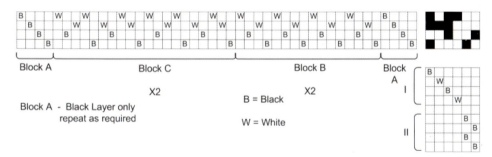

Figure 7-8b. Draft for plain weave supplementary warp joined by exchanging layers

then it pulls in again when the layers are separate again. In the attached areas, the white upper layer is left unwoven where it exchanges with the lower layer. The fabric is different on both sides.

To follow the threading draft, Block A is repeated as necessary to the required width to give the black single layer on each side of the supplementary warp. Then thread the white and black layer, with Blocks B and C alternately, for the desired width. In the treadling, Block I weaves the two layers separately, with Block II weaving the joined sections for four picks.

The draft in Figure 7-8a and for Photo 7-8 is woven in 2/2 twill and requires a loom with 12 treadles, so it can only be woven on an eight-shaft table loom or an eight-shaft dobby loom. An alternative, if you have a loom with an easy method of changing the treadle to shaft tie-up, is to re-tie four treadles when weaving Block II, the block that is woven only when the layers are joined. A simpler version, in plain weave, Figure 7-8b, needs only four shafts and six treadles.

Supplementary warp with floats (Figure 7-9)

In this supplementary warp pattern, the white layer is left unwoven, and moves under and over the black layer. The fabric is the same on both sides.

Collapse Weave

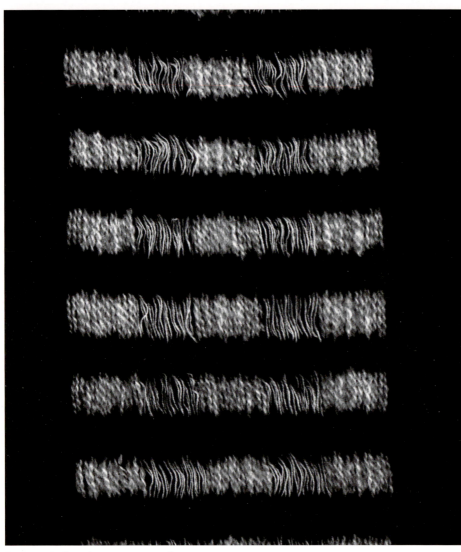

Photo 7-9. Supplementary warp floats.

Supplementary warp in elastic yarns

Some elastic yarns are easier to work with than others. Some lie straight until washed and these are easier to handle. Others rebound as soon as tension is released. The former are easier to handle but both types can be used. Lycra is the common name for most elastic yarns.

Putting a warp on with an elastic yarn is not as difficult as it sounds. Two separate warps are necessary because of the extreme variation between the base and the elastic warp. These two warps need to be beamed or weighted separately, as described on pages 68-71. Attach a length of sticky tape to the loom and when you are threading the heddles push each elastic warp end onto the tape as soon as it emerges from the heddles. This keeps the elastic warp under control. Once the elastic yarn is under tension it behaves itself. In the following samples the six outside elastic yarns on each selvedge are doubled in the heddles to give added take-up.

The ends of the weaving need to be hemmed before washing. A fringe looks rather peculiar as the elastic yarn makes the supplementary section of the fringe much shorter than the rest. For this hem, weave one inch in 2/2 twill or plain weave (whichever weave matches the body of the work) at the beginning and end of each piece as in Block I of the treadling draft. Hem stitch the ends while the cloth is still

Eight- to Sixteen-shaft Double Weave and Supplementary Warps

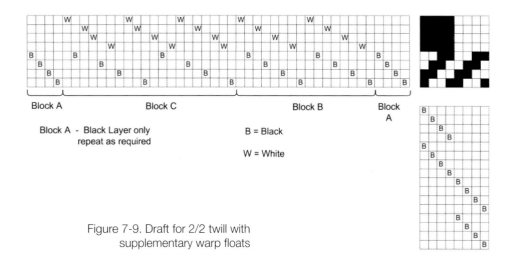

Figure 7-9. Draft for 2/2 twill with supplementary warp floats

on the loom then, after removing it from the loom, turn the hem under and sew by hand before washing.

Weaving the elastic supplementary warp in floats, where the supplementary warp is alternately above and below the base weave, is similar to the technique used in Figure 7-9. A four-shaft loom can be used when the base warp is threaded on the first two shafts and the supplementary ends are threaded on Shafts 3 and 4. Only plain weave can be woven on two shafts. Six or eight shafts are needed for twills.

The base layer should be fine and flexible to allow for gathering and puckering when pulled up by the elastic supplementary warp. The following samples used a 2/20 silk for the base warp, sett at 20 epi, and were woven with the same weft yarn in a balanced weave at 20 ppi. The elastic warp was a grey elastic Lycra yarn, also sett at 20 epi. The warp was 9in (23cm) wide, with the supplementary warp 3in (8cm) wide, placed in the center. The width can be adjusted to suit by threading Blocks A, B (supplementary warp), and C as required. In the treadling draft Block I weaves the section that will be hemmed when off the loom, Block II has the supplementary warp on the surface, and Block III the supplementary warp on the underside of the weaving (Figure 7-10a).

Because this is a one-shuttle weave the weaving is fast, which is just as well because the amount of take-up of the base warp, when washed and gathered by the elastic warp,

Collapse Weave

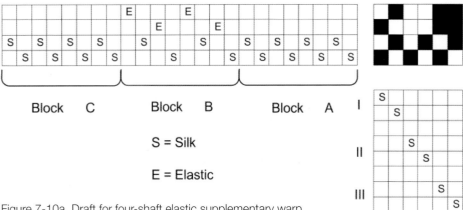

Figure 7-10a. Draft for four-shaft elastic supplementary warp

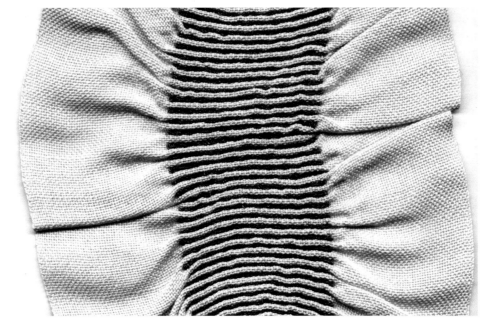

Photo 7-10a. A four-shaft elastic supplementary warp.

Eight- to Sixteen-shaft Double Weave and Supplementary Warps

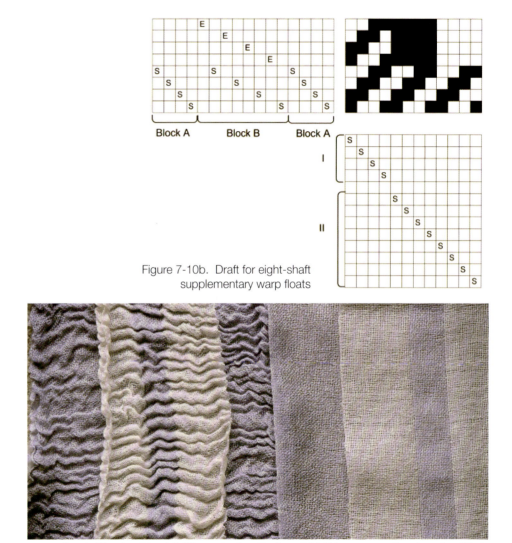

Figure 7-10b. Draft for eight-shaft supplementary warp floats

Scarf. 'Fleeting Clouds'. Woven by Sue Foulkes, UK. Warp: over-twisted merino. Weft: botany lambswool/silk yarn. Double weave. Photographer Martin Foulkes.

Collapse Weave

is approximately 50 per cent. To weave a scarf 5ft (1.5m) in length, you would need to weave approximately 7.5ft (2.25m). Sampling is recommended because elastic yarns will shrink at different rates. This eight-shaft version (7-10b), with a background in 2/2 twill, needs only eight treadles for the body of the cloth, but an extra four treadles for the hem (Block I). This can be done by retying the treadles for Block I, as before. To follow the threading draft, Block A has the silk on its own on Shafts 1-4, Block B has the silk on Shafts 1-4 and the elastic yarn on Shafts 5-8, both layers sett at 20 epi.

Block I of the treadling draft weaves the hem, Block II the body of the weaving.

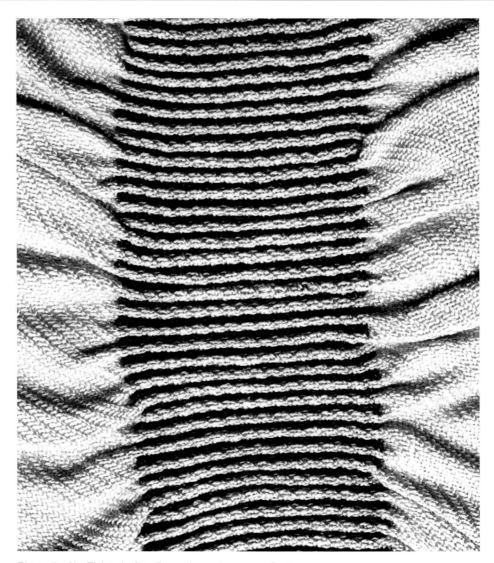

Photo 7-10b. Eight-shaft twill supplementary warp floats.

Eight- to Sixteen-shaft Double Weave and Supplementary Warps

Scarves. Woven by Win Currie, New Zealand. Double weave scarves in silk and wool. Photographer Edward Field.

Scarf. Woven and photographed by Sandra Rude, USA. Silk base cloth with merino supplementary warp on reverse, tied down only at merino weft stripes.

Collapse Weave

Scarves. Woven by Brigit Howitt, New Zealand. Silk and lycra with supplementary warp. Photographer Jurgen Jenner.

Eight- to Sixteen-shaft Double Weave and Supplementary Warps

Scarf. Woven and photographed by Sandra Rude, USA. Double weave with painted silk and grey wool layers.

8 Bumps, Lumps and Spaces

This chapter covers factors that cause the fabric to bulge and pull in and out, sometimes all in the same piece of cloth. It is the different yarn qualities that makes these lumps and bumps. Previous chapters have been written about fabrics that pleat or fold in the warp or weft. The same factors that cause this pleating can also achieve other very interesting results.

SHRINKAGE

Shrinkage is the ability of the yarns to swell and increase in size as well as contract in length. Chapter Three covers this in detail. The yarn sett plays a large part by allowing some of the yarns to move and some to remain in place. This movement forces the more stable areas into humps and bumps. The secret of weaving bumps and lumps is in the sett and beating, as well as the structure. The shrinkable yarns need to be loosely sett and beaten, to allow plenty of movement. A general rule is that the shrinkable yarns should be sett at about one half to one third of the normal balanced, plain weave sett. If the shrinkable yarns are sett too close, they will still shrink, but not as much as required and will make a very firm, inflexible felted cloth when washed. The stable, non-shrinking yarns should be sett and beaten firmly to give very little movement when washed. The size of the squares and stripes also make a difference. If they are too small, the yarns will not react against each other. Too large and the pull the different yarns exert is dissipated. Test for shrinkage by following the instructions on page 24.

Over the years I have been researching collapse fabrics I have collected a strange assortment of yarns of the kind that most normal weavers would avoid. Sometimes I pick these up in factory seconds bins; some were given to me by other weavers who found these yarns doing unexpected things when woven and finished. Because the yarns used in some of the samples in this chapter are 'orphans', they are not in the suppliers list. I will describe the size of these yarns and the yarns I have had spun to order in wraps per inch. This is worked out by winding the yarn around a ruler for one inch so each thread is touching the adjacent one, then counting the number of wraps around the ruler. This is not the sett of the yarn, purely the size.

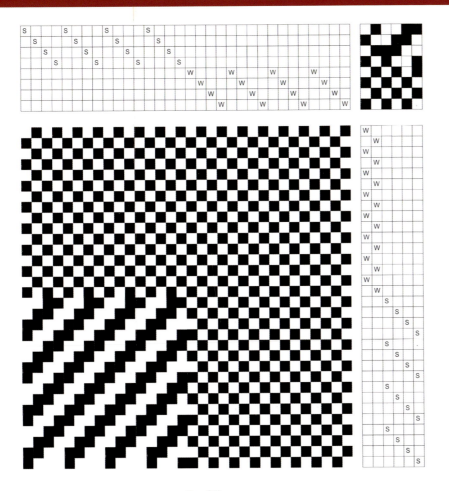

Silk and wool squares

A simple example of how two different yarns react when washed is shown in Photo 8-1. The unshrinkable silk squares in a 2/2 twill, sett at 20 epi, are surrounded by a shrinkable wool, sett at 20 epi in plain weave. Repeat the draft as required but finish with a wool square. When it is washed in the full cycle of the washing machine the wool shrinks around the silk squares. Weaving the silk squares in 2/2 twill rather than plain weave gives them more flexibility and increases the puffiness. Tencel and rayon could also be used in place of silk. Using shiny and dull yarns, as in this sample, adds to the contrast. Because the wool is sett with the same epi as the silk, the wool squares have felted. For a softer, lighter fabric the wool squares could be sett at half that of the silk.

S = Silk
W = Wool

Figure 8-1. Draft for silk and wool squares

Collapse Weave

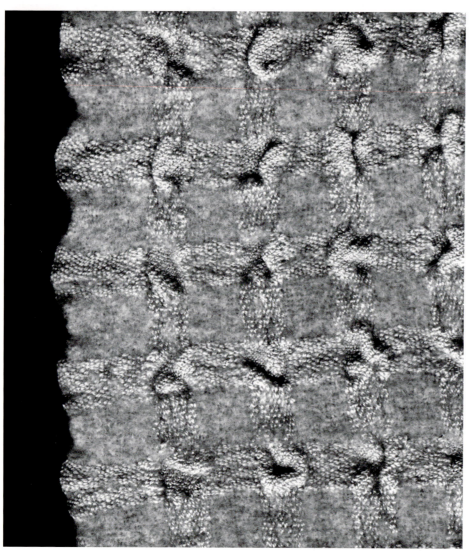

Photo 8-1. Silk and wool fabric.

Basket weave (Photo 8-2)

In this sample I have again used silk as the non-shrinkable yarn but used a possum/merino blend yarn, which shrinks very easily, for the shrinkable squares. This yarn, which is 37 per cent possum fur, 60 per cent merino wool and 3 per cent nylon, shrinks 25-30 per cent when washed. This is a new yarn, made only in New Zealand, where we have 70 million possums to get rid of. (They look cute but they are pests, so everyone was delighted when a sensible use was found for the fur.) This yarn is listed in the suppliers list. In the center of the silk squares I have added a basket weave square. Plain weave was used for both the silk and possum/merino squares. The possum/merino yarn was sett at 5 epi and the silk at 20 epi. The picks per inch were the same as the sett. Block A of the threading draft (Figure 8-2), was threaded twice (16 ends) to form one square, and Block B threaded once (40 ends). Repeat the blocks as required, but finish with an A block. The squares were 2in (5cm) wide on the loom. Finish this sample by washing it in the regular cycle of the washing machine with hot water to achieve maximum shrinkage.

Bumps, Lumps and Spaces

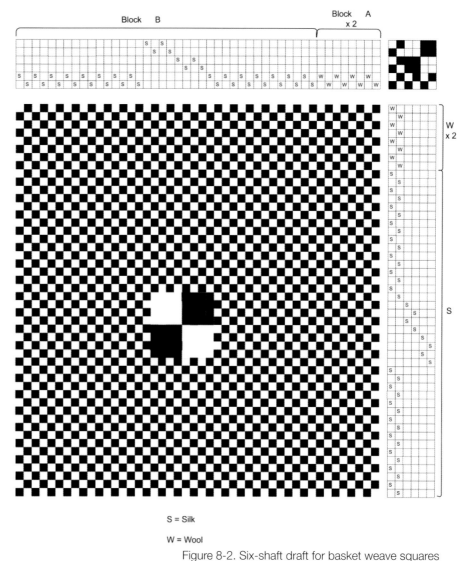

S = Silk
W = Wool

Figure 8-2. Six-shaft draft for basket weave squares

Collapse Weave

Photo 8-2. Six-shaft basket weave squares.

DEFLECTED DOUBLE WEAVE

This is an ideal weave structure for making bumpy cloth because the warp and weft yarns can be of different types and sett and woven open or close together to allow the yarns to move or remain stable. By exaggerating this difference and using some yarns that will shrink and some that will not, very interesting effects can be woven.

Deflected double weave is a two-layer cloth, with parts of one layer exchanging with the other to form patterns in both layers. Some of the warp and weft yarns float over each other, and this causes the deflection when the yarns move when washed. The front and back sides are different.

The non-shrinkable yarn used in the warp and weft for this sample was 10/2 Tencel yarn. The warp yarn was a black, shrinkable 110/2 wool; the weft yarn was a black possum/merino yarn, as described in the previous sample. Any wool yarn that shrinks could be used in place of the possum/merino yarn.

If you examine the draft figure 8-3, you will see that the Tencel blocks on Shafts 3, 4, 7 and 8 are twice as long as the wool blocks on Shafts 1 and 2, 5 and 6. The Tencel blocks are also sett closer together at 24 epi; the wool blocks are sett at 6 epi.

Bumps, Lumps and Spaces

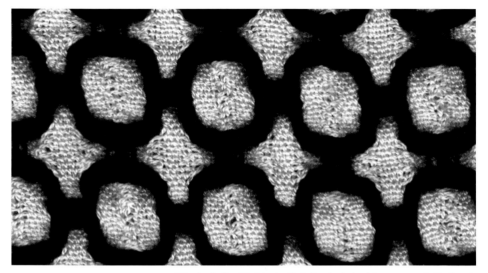

Photo 8-3a. Eight-shaft deflected double weave cloth, front.

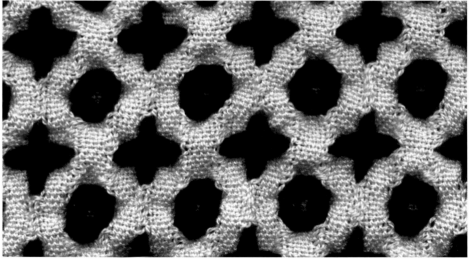

Photo 8-3b. Eight-shaft deflected double weave cloth, back.

To achieve a neat selvedge, finish with a Tencel block at each selvedge. Picks per inch are the same as the sett, which means that the Tencel blocks are solid and closely beaten, while the wool is allowed room to move. Two shuttles were used, one with the black yarn and one with the white. For tidy selvedges, the shuttle with the black yarn is not taken to the outside edges but brought up at the end of the last black ends.

Deflected double weave looks odd on the loom because it is not until the cloth is washed and the yarns move, that the final effect is seen. The sample in Photos 8-3a and 8-3b was washed in the full cycle of the washing machine.

There are many other drafts for deflected double weave that can be adapted for collapse weave cloth, remembering the golden rule of setting the shrinkable areas wider than the others.

Collapse Weave

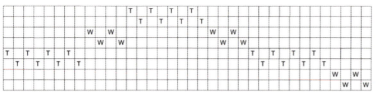

T = Tencel

W = Wool

Figure 8-3. Eight-shaft draft for deflected double weave

TRACKING AND FELTING

Tracking is shown in Photo 3-2b. In that sample the tracking was accidental and I ruined several scarves, but fortunately I seem to learn more from my mistakes than I do when I get things right first time. In this sample (Photo 8-4), using the same brown alpaca yarn as in Photo 3-2b and a white wool singles, the warp was sett very loosely and the weft was beaten lightly. Both the alpaca and wool yarns were sett at 8 epi and the weft beaten in at 8 ppi. The normal sett for a balanced plain weave in these yarns would normally be twice as much. The alpaca yarn was a singles, unbalanced yarn sized at 20 wraps per inch. The wool singles was sized at 26 wraps per inch and was a softer yarn. Both these yarns I had custom spun for me.

The sample was woven with 4in (10cm) squares of the alpaca and wool alternately, outlined by two strands of a grey wool bouclé (14 wraps per inch). This bouclé was one of my 'orphan' yarns, given to me because it shrank so much that a weaving friend found it impossible to use. The weaving was plain weave.

After it was washed in the full cycle of the washing machine the change was dramatic. The alpaca squares tracked beautifully and were surrounded by the felted wool singles squares. The squares with an alpaca weft and a wool warp

Bumps, Lumps and Spaces

Photo 8-4. Tracking and felting.

formed vertical pleats; the squares with an alpaca warp and a wool weft formed horizontal pleats. It was a most interesting effect. To most weavers, tracking is a mistake that should be avoided, but to me it makes a fascinating cloth.

Collapse Weave

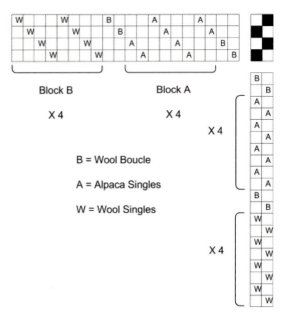

Figure 8-4. Draft for tracked and felted cloth.

GATHERING

An easy method of making lumps and bumps is to gather the cloth after it has been woven, but before washing. This is such a simple idea, that I am surprised it is not used more often. Two types of yarns are needed. One is a strong gathering yarn, added at intervals in the warp, and the other a soft yarn that will gather easily. For the strong gathering yarn a slippery yarn such as rayon, Tencel, mercerized cotton or silk is best. For the background a soft yarn such as wool, unmercerized cotton or mohair can be used. In the following sample I used a rayon ribbon for the gathered warp threads and 110/2 wool yarn for the rest of the warp and for the weft. A 2/2 twill makes a soft, flexible cloth that will gather easily.

Remember to weave more than usual, because the cloth shortens dramatically when gathered. For a tightly-gathered cloth, this take-up in length could be as much as 50 per cent. For a lightly-gathered cloth, the take-up would be about 25 per cent.

The 3/1 twill sample was interesting: by weaving with a contrasting purple weft, one side was black and the other purple. The warp was wound as follows:
Straight draw (1, 2, 3, 4) with 44 ends of black 110/2 wool, two ends rayon ribbon, 32 ends of wool, one end of rayon, 32 black,

Bumps, Lumps and Spaces

Photo 8-5a. Gathered sample in 2/2 twill

Photo 8-5b. Gathered sample in 3/1 twill

Collapse Weave

two rayon, 32 black, one rayon, 44 ends black. The sett was 16 epi for the black, with two ends in each dent of an eight-dent reed and with the rayon spaced singly in a dent. It was woven with 16 ppi. After removing the weaving from the loom and before washing, the rayon ribbons were pulled through the wool warp to form the gathers and the ends of the ribbon tied in a knot to prevent the gathers undoing. The sample was then washed.

The gathering warp ends can be placed together in the center of the warp, giving almost the same effect as a supplementary warp, and then pulled up.

FLOATS

By leaving unwoven areas in the warp or weft or both, pleats and folds in the cloth can be exaggerated. With eight shafts, as in the draft in Figure 8-6, the floats can cover portions of the cloth only. In these samples the first four shafts were threaded in one-inch stripes of 110/2 wool sett at 16 epi, as in Block A in the draft, then Shafts 5–8 in 56/2 wool were sett at 24 epi for Block B. Using the thinner wool allows more flexibility in the pleats. To weave Sample 8-6a, 3in (7.5cm) were woven with the 110/2 as the weft in plain weave, as in Block I in the draft, then 12 picks in a wool/Lycra blend yarn, as in Block II, with 16 ppi. Thus the elastic yarn floats over

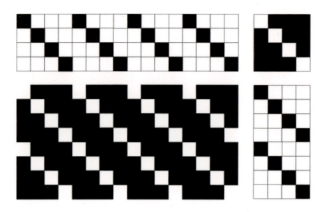

Figure 8-5. Draft for gathered weave in 3/1 twill

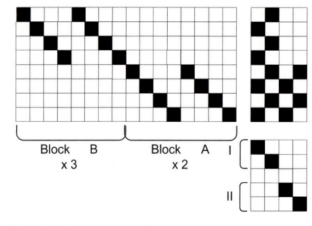

Figure 8-6. Draft for spaced floats

Bumps, Lumps and Spaces

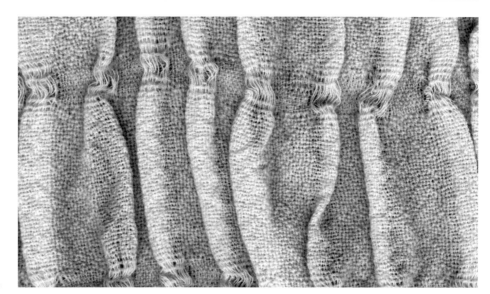

Photo 8-6a. Spaced floats

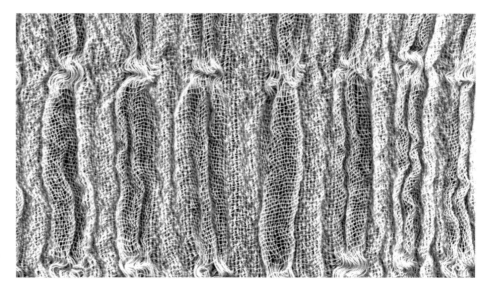

Photo 8-6b. Spaced floats with a weft of 56/2 over-twisted wool

Collapse Weave

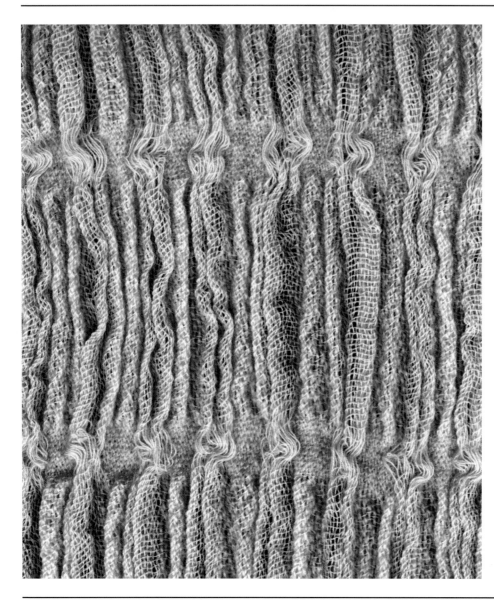

Photo 8-6c. Spaced floats with an elastic weft.

the warp on the 56/2 stripes. If the warp is wound with half-inch stripes, the pleating is tighter.

Following the same draft, the sample in Photo 8-6b was woven with 56/2 as the weft for both the plain weave areas and the floats and beaten with 16 ppi. The over-twisted wool weft has pulled in considerably more than the 110/2 wool and wool/Lycra blend weft in 8-6a. In Sample 8-6b, as well, the over-twisted wool curls and kinks up in the floats.

In Photo 8-6c the weft used was wool/Lycra for both the floats and the body of the weaving, giving tighter and more even pleating.

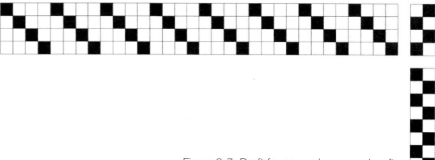

Figure 8-7. Draft for spaced warp and weft.

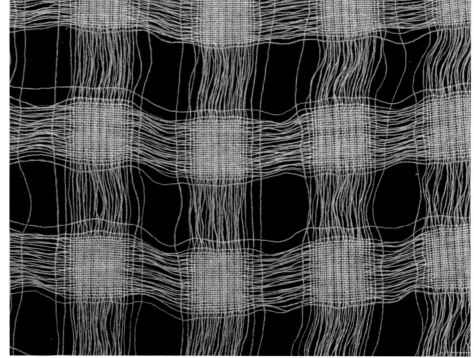

Photo 8-7a. Spaced warp and weft, before finishing.

Collapse Weave

SPACED WARP AND WEFT

Spacing the warp and weft, using an over-twisted yarn for both, creates interesting areas of contrast. The yarn that floats over the spaces will twist and curl when finished, while the plain weave areas remain flat and stable.

In Photo 8-7a the warp and weft were 56/2 over-twisted wool and the woven areas were sett at 32 epi. With an eight-dent reed, four ends were placed in each dent for an inch, eight dents left empty, then the next eight were threaded with four ends each, and so on across the width.

Weave 32 picks for one inch in plain weave, then place a smooth stick one inch wide in the next shed, change sheds again, then weave another 32 picks. The stick can be gently removed after five or six picks. Again, when it was finished the contraction was 25 per cent in both width and length.

I finished this sample by soaking it in boiling water for a few minutes, because I thought the agitation when washing would disturb the long floats. The change was dramatic; as soon as the cloth touched the boiling water it gathered itself up in curls and folds. Steaming would have had the same effect.

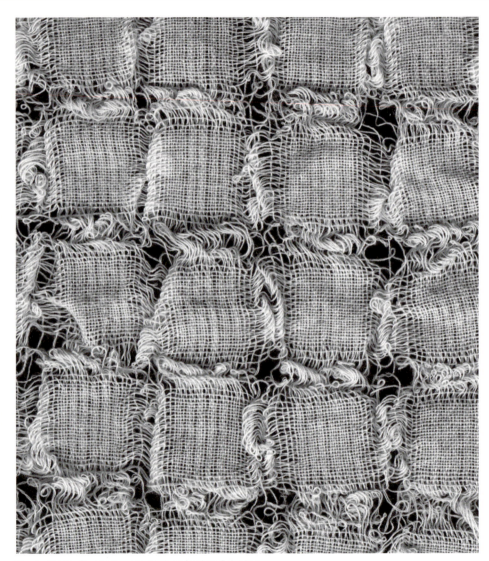

Photo 8-7b. Spaced warp and weft after finishing.

Bumps, Lumps and Spaces

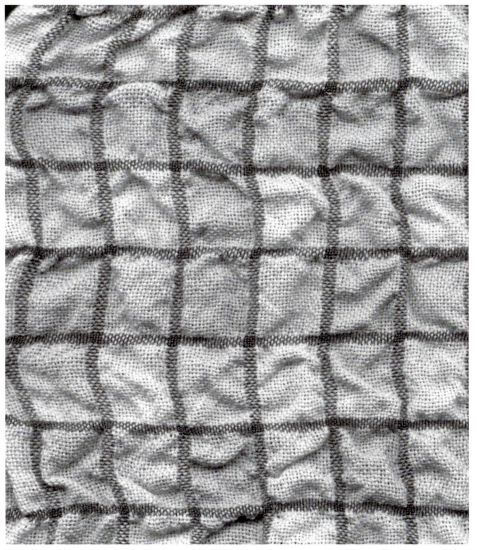

Photo 8-8. Gathered squares

GATHERED SQUARES

The sample in Photo 8-8 was woven in plain weave, as in Figure 8-7, with the elastic yarn that outlined each square pulling the cloth into puckers. The main yarn used was fine enough to allow the puckering to take place after washing. A thick yarn requires a thicker and stronger elastic thread. In this sample I chose a 70 per cent cotton/30 per cent wool blend yarn sett at 24 epi. Both the warp and the weft had one-inch blocks in two colors separated by four strands of a grey elastic yarn. Lycra and colcolastic (a cotton and elastic blend) yarns are both suitable for the elastic threads. The elastic warp yarns are no problem and do not need to be beamed separately.

Collapse Weave

Samples of fabric. Woven by Helen Fry, UK. Yellow sample: lambswool, alpaca and botany yarn, dyed with acid dyes, plain weave, tied using shibori techniques and washed on normal 40° domestic wash. Blue/white sample: 100% lambswool, plain weave, tied using shibori techniques and washed on normal 40° domestic wash. Photographer David Fry.

Scarf. Woven and photographed by Sandra Rude, USA. Grey merino and white wool/Tencel. Before and after washing.

Bumps, Lumps and Spaces

Scarf. 'Organized Chaos'.
Woven and photographed by
Sheila Reimann, New Zealand.
50% wool, 50% silk.

Scarf. 'Bubble Wrap'.
Woven and photographed by Sheila
Reimann, New Zealand.
100% wool.

Collapse Weave

Sample. Woven by Helen Fry, UK. Shetland and botany wool, woven in plain weave, tied using shibori techniques, dyed using direct dyes, then washed twice in normal 40° domestic wash.
Photographer David Fry.

Scarf. 'Cross Currents'.
Woven by Fran Regan, Australia. Two-ply merino wool and Waverley Mill singles, layered.
Photographer Barry Regan.

Bumps, Lumps and Spaces

Scarf. Woven by Helen Fry, UK. 100% lambswool, woven in plain weave, tied using shibori techniques, washed three times in a normal 40° domestic wash.
Photographer David Fry.

9 Odds and Ends

The more I researched collapse weave and talked to others who were also exploring this subject, the more ideas we came up with. This chapter covers some interesting techniques that do not seem to fit into anywhere else.

FELTED FLOATS

If you weave with soft, shrinkable wool and can steel yourself to put your beautiful weaving through the full cycle of the washing machine, interesting things happen. The woven areas, if sett close enough, will not felt much, but any unwoven areas, such as floats, will shrink and in doing so, pull the weaving in. After several failures, I found that the floats need to be at least 1 1/2 inches (4cm) long to felt properly. However, the sample in Photo 9-1a, which has one-inch floats, produced an interesting cloth with dimples in it. Because the floats adhere to the cloth surface, the floats will not pull out and snag.

Six shafts are necessary because an extra two shafts are needed for the edges. The floats cannot continue right up to the selvedges because this makes them unsightly. Blocks B and C in the threading draft can be repeated as many times as you wish. Block A is the selvedge block and this can be made wider.

Photo 9-1a. Felted floats

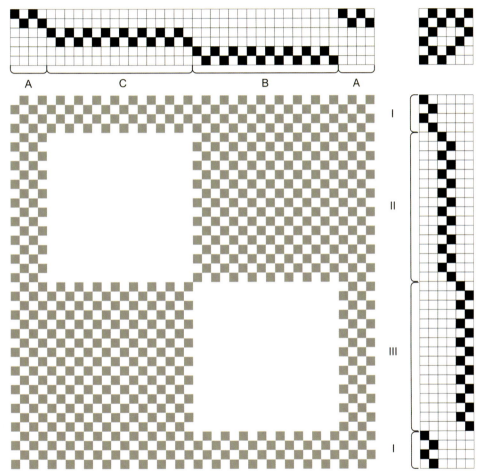

Figure 9-1a. Draft for six-shaft felted floats

The warp and weft were both 110/2, a shrinkable merino sett and woven with 16 epi. Any other soft, shrinkable wool will give the same effect and should be sett for a balanced plain weave. The shrinkage rate was 25 per cent when the sample was washed in the full cycle of the washing machine. One side has warp floats, the other weft floats.

Basket weave floats

With this draft (Figure 9-1b) the floats pass under and over each other. The original floats were 2in (5cm) long but they reduced to 1 1/2in (4cm) with washing. The floats separated into two or three sections when they were felted by washing in the full cycle of the washing machine. This structure is intriguing because the floats 'weave' under and over, resembling basket weave.

Again the warp was 110/2 shrinkable merino, sett and woven at 16 epi. When threading, Blocks A, B, and C were repeated in that order, finishing with an A block. The weft was woven in the same order. The borders between the float areas can be extended (Blocks A and I) and this will give larger pockets of plain weave in between the floats. As with Figure 9-1a, six shafts are necessary because two extra shafts are needed for the selvedges.

Collapse Weave

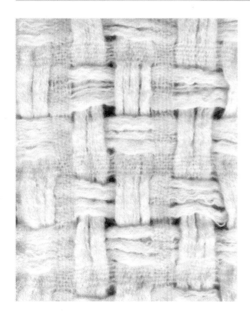

Photo 9-1b. Basket weave felted floats

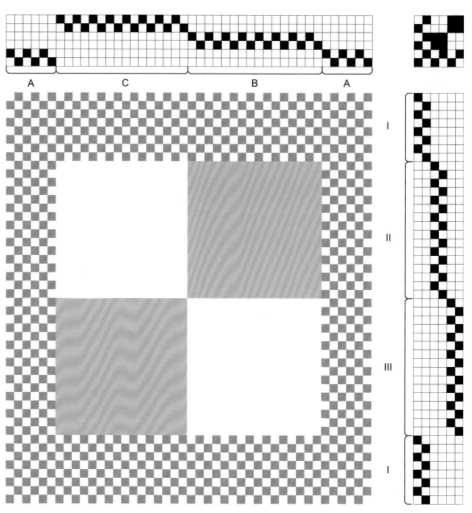

Figure 9-1b. Draft for six-shaft basket weave felted floats

Odds and Ends

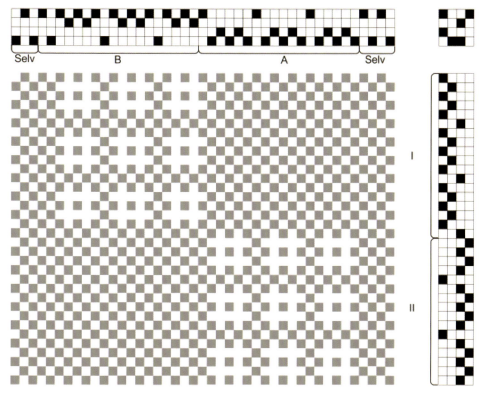

Figure 9-2. Draft for Swedish lace

SWEDISH LACE

Because this pattern (Figure 9-2) has blocks of floats alternating with blocks of plain weave, the float blocks pull in when washed forming an interesting surface pattern. The warp is the 56/2 over-twisted wool, sett at 32 epi to form a balanced plain weave in the plain areas. When the weft is the same as the warp, the plain weave areas form pockets and pouches in the pleats, as can be seen in Photo 9-2a. When the weft is a wool/Lycra blend, the plain weave areas form vertical pleats, and the pattern areas with weft floats form horizontal pleats on the upper side, as in Photo 9-2b. The underneath has both plain and pattern areas forming vertical pleats. The weft was woven with 32 ppi.

Collapse Weave

Photo 9-2a. Swedish lace with same weft as warp

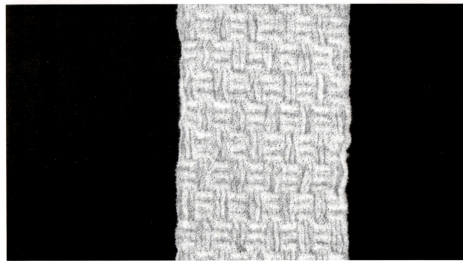

Photo 9-2b. Swedish lace with elastic weft

OVERSHOT WEAVE

Overshot patterns are woven with a pattern weft, which floats over the background areas, and a background weft, usually the same as the warp, which forms a plain weave background. This background plain weave is called a tabby binder. It is not usually shown on drafts, because it would make them too long, but the instructions with the drafts will indicate the binder weft. The binder is usually woven alternately on Shafts 1 and 3, and 2 and 4, with one of these background picks between each pattern pick.

There are many overshot patterns that would form interesting collapse fabrics. I have chosen two to include in this chapter as examples. One is a block pattern and the other a diamond pattern. The pattern areas can cover the complete cloth, or part of it to form borders. As these borders will pull in more than the body of the cloth, they can form interesting borders on scarves, wraps or garments. These overshot samples were all woven with 110/2 merino wool warp sett at 16 epi. The background weft was the same as the warp.

Odds and Ends

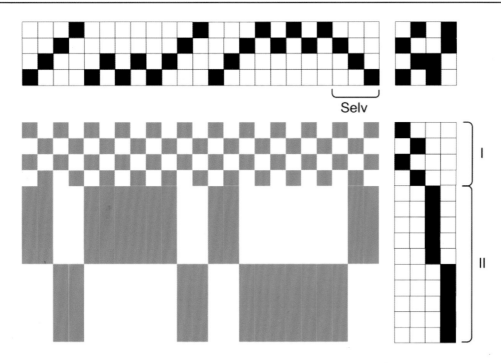

I = Plain weave
II = Pattern area weave with plain weave binder.

Figure 9-3. Draft for Miniature Monk's belt

Worms

An important factor that came to the fore when weaving these overshot patterns was the 'worms' that the pattern weft sometimes formed on the cloth surface. When the cloth contracts, the spare weft has to go somewhere. If the yarn is very over-twisted, as with 1/30 wool, when the cloth contracts in width, the weft yarn has nowhere to go and pops up on the surface in little loops ('worms'). This detracts from the surface of the cloth, as can be seen in Photo 9-3a and Photo 3-4.

If it is an elastic weft such as Lycra there is no problem because the elasticity of the yarn allows it to expand and contract within the yarn itself (Photo 9-3b).

Collapse Weave

Miniature Monk's belt

The sample in Photo 9-3b was woven with stripes of Lycra pattern weft at 32 ppi, which did not worm. The background weft was woven with 16 ppi. However, when the entire surface was woven with a Lycra pattern weft and the background weft both sett at 32 ppi, as in Photo 9-3c, the fabric felt harsh. Photo 9-3d shows a sample woven with the same yarns but at 16 ppi it had a much softer handle.

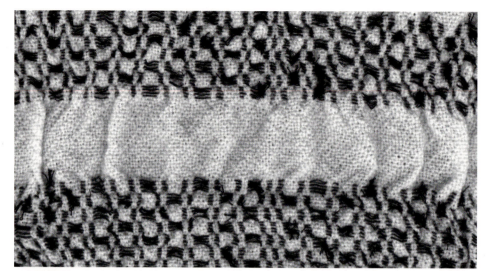

Photo 9-3a. Miniature Monk's belt. Weft stripes with over-twisted pattern weft

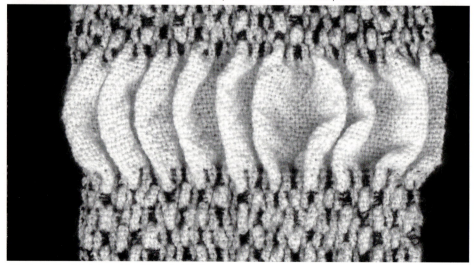

Photo 9-3b. Miniature Monk's belt. Weft stripes in Lycra

Odds and Ends

Italian diamond

This sample was woven with 110/2 wool warp sett at 16 epi and background weft of the same yarn, with Lycra as the pattern weft at 32 ppi. There are many variations of this, as with the previous block pattern. The pattern can be woven in weft stripes separated by contrasting areas of plain weave or it can be woven with 16 ppi to make a softer cloth.

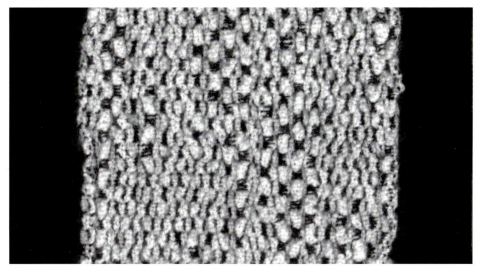

Photo 9-3c. Miniature Monk's Belt with Lycra weft at 32 ppi

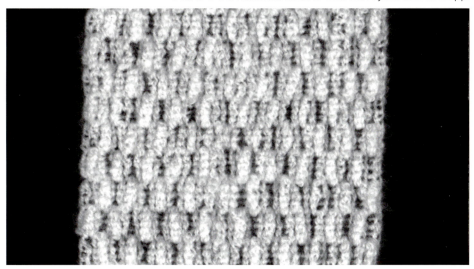

Photo 9-3d. Miniature Monk's belt with Lycra weft at 16 ppi

Collapse Weave

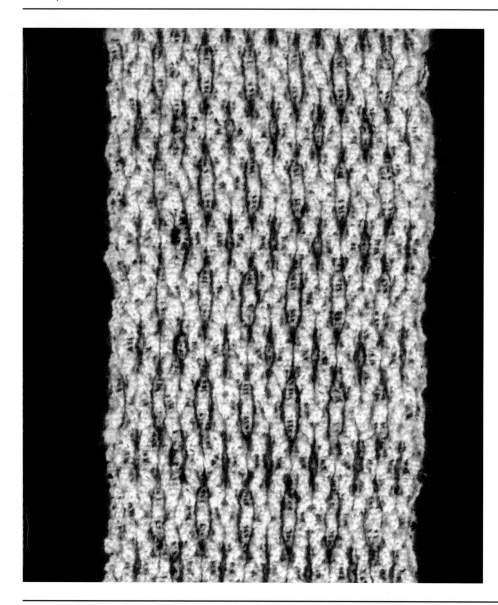

Photo 9-4. Italian diamomd with Lycra pattern weft

Odds and Ends

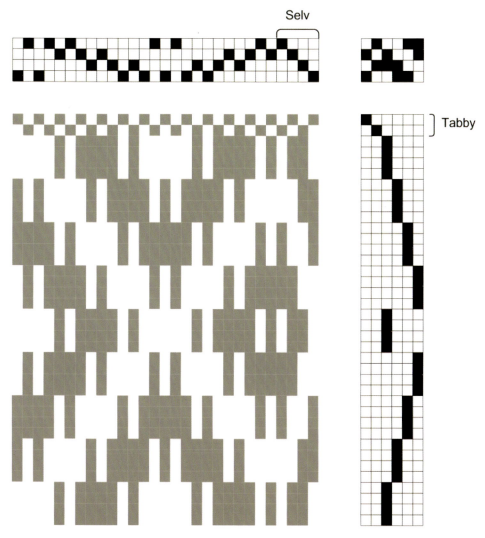

Figure 9-4. Draft for Italian diamond

DIAGONAL TWILL

This is an eight-shaft draft. The sample was woven with tripled black 30/1 over-twisted wool as the weft and 110/2 wool for the warp. The surface forms vertical pleats but with the pleats showing a definite twill line forming smaller, secondary diagonal pleats.

Remember that the finer yarns can be doubled or tripled or more to become thicker warp or weft yarns. The sample was sett at 16 epi and woven with 32 ppi.

Collapse Weave

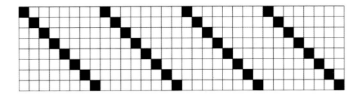

Figure 9-5. Draft for diagonal twill

Odds and Ends

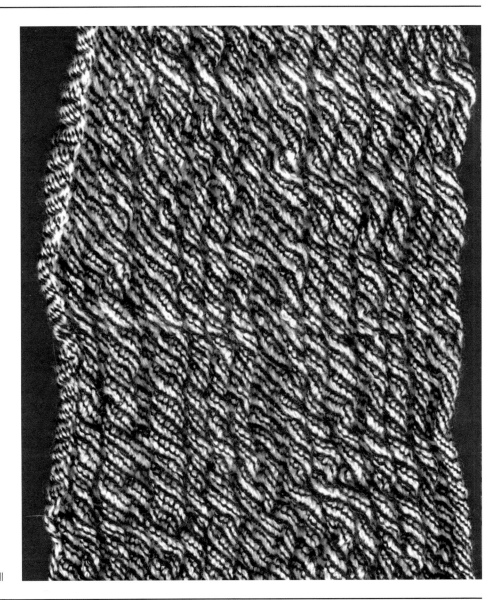

Photo 9-5. Diagonal twill

Collapse Weave

HUCKABACK

As the structure of huckaback has floats – weft floats on one side and warp floats on the other – I thought the texture would be interesting when the floats were woven in the over-twisted yarn. The warp had the 110/2 shrinkable wool on Shafts 1 and 4, with the 56/2 over-twisted wool on Shafts 2 and 3, sett at 16 epi.

The weft was also woven with both yarns. In the upper sample (Photo 9-6) Lycra was used instead of the 56/2 in the weft only. This caused the sample to pull in more and emphasize the texture. It was woven with 16 ppi and both the Lyrca and the wool weft produced a very soft handle.

Photo 9-6. Huckaback

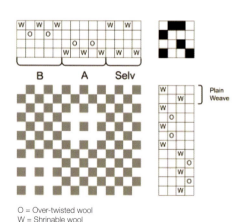

O = Over-twisted wool
W = Shrinable wool

Figure 9-6. Draft for huckaback.

Odds and Ends

Photo 9-7a. Advancing twill

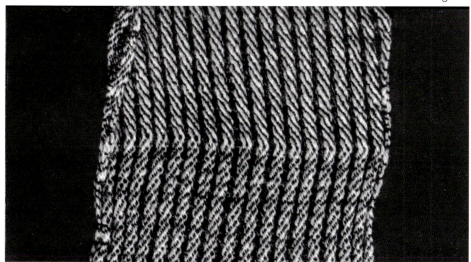

Photo 9-7b. Reversing the diagonal twill lines

ADVANCING TWILL

This is a 16-shaft draft. The warp for this sample was the white 110/2 shrinkable wool and the weft was a black elastic yarn. By advancing the five-end twill across one warp end at a time while weaving, the uniform pleats form a diagonal line, with eight warp ends in each of the stripes. As each stripe is either a 1/3 twill (almost a weft-face cloth) or a 3/1 twill (warp-face cloth) each stripe either recedes or advances, forming the pleats.

In Photo 9-7b, the twill direction is reversed at regular intervals.

There are many other patterns that can be utilized to add structure to collapse cloth and I have included only a few in this chapter. As I wove the samples for this chapter, I had to decide where to stop, because each new pattern led me to think of others.

Collapse Weave

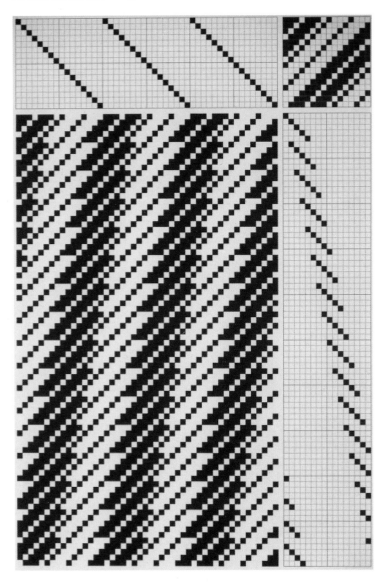

Figure 9-7. Draft for advancing twill.

Odds and Ends

Scarf.
Woven and photographed by
Sandra Rude, USA.
Silk warp and weft, turned satin on
networked curve.

10 Projects

As my knowledge of collapse weave grew, so did my appreciation of the range of articles that could be made from this cloth. I can make simple garments myself, but for more complex outfits I rely on my fashion designer, Sylvia Campbell. Some of these up-market fashion garments are shown throughout the book and I hope they will provide inspiration for you. However, in this chapter, I will describe how to make easy garments that reflect the nature of the cloth itself. In most of the following garments there is minimal cutting required. It is the flowing, flexible and soft handle of the cloth that determines the finished garment. The cloth seems to have a life of its own. It bounces and moves with the movement of the body and this is reflected in the following projects. I am sure you will think of other ways to use this fabric but these ideas may just start you thinking.

All the measurements are for the *finished* articles, because the width and length will alter so dramatically with the washing of the different yarns and the techniques used in the weaving. A loss of 50 per cent in the cloth width after removing it from the loom and washing was the norm in most of my samples. Some collapse fabrics contract more in the width than the length and some do the opposite, so weave some samples first. Another point to remember is that the cloth collapses more in narrow widths, therefore the maximum width I weave on my loom is 22 ins (55cm), which gives me about 8-10 ins (20-25cm) when finished. All the fabric pieces that make up garments in this chapter are of this width. When I need finished pieces that are wider I stitch them together by hand; this join does not show amongst the pleating. Hand sewing is strong enough and is invisible if you butt the edges together and use a matching yarn.

All the sizes in these projects can be adjusted. The dotted lines in the drawings show the sewing measurements.

FINISHING

I finish most of my collapse cloth in the washing machine. Because of the agitation this involves, the ends have to be strong and finished in some way before washing. I usually twist the fringe. Another finish is to hemstitch on the loom, wash the cloth, then stretch the hemstitched end and over-sew it several times with a zig zag stitch on the sewing machine. This leaves a wavy frou-frou at the end. Make sure the stitch zigs and zags over the outside edge because this prevents fraying. Stitching several rounds gives the edge a

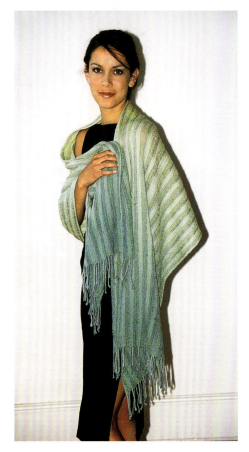

Dyed wrap. Woven by Anne Field, New Zealand. 56/2 over-twisted merino wool, 110/2 shrinkable merino wool, woven in 2/2 twill. Dyed with fiber-reactive dyes. Photographer Edward Field.

Wrap. Woven by Jane Clark, New Zealand. Cotton and colcolastic warp and weft. Photographer Tony Clark.

firm finish and pushes the frou frou out. Several of the garments Sylvia has made for me have this finish.

It is not advisable to just hemstitch, then wash. The fringe tangles, especially if you have used an over-twisted yarn for some of the warp ends. Also one type of yarn often ends up shorter than the other because the shrinkage rates are different.

Dyeing is best done after the collapse is completed (see page 45).

SCARVES

This is the most obvious use of the fabric because the pleats and puckers, which are usually vertical, make a comfortable scarf that hangs well. I weave most of my scarves so they will be 5-6ft (150-180cm) long and 8-10in (20-25cm) wide when finished. However, there are so many ways of wearing a scarf that the length and width can vary. Some like a long narrow scarf that can be folded in two lengthwise with both ends put through the loop, others like a short scarf that just hangs down the front, while others like a very long scarf that will wind a couple of times around the neck or with the two ends thrown over both shoulders.

Collapse Weave

WRAPS

Two narrow widths collapse better than one wide piece, so join two lengths of cloth together lengthwise, to make the finished wrap wide enough. Weave two lengths with a finished length of 7ft (210cm) and width of 8-10in (20-25cm) wide. The join will not be obvious.

STRAIGHT TOP

Two widths, 8-10in (20-25cm) wide and 40in (102cm) long, make up this simple top. The center back is joined for 12in (30cm) and the underarm seams are joined together for 6in (15cm). Do not join the front edges. One fringe tie on each waist end can be tied together to hold the two fronts together. Because most of us are a different shape at the front compared to the back, sewing the front sides together causes the front to ride up. This can be disguised by leaving a longer fringe at the front edges and trimming them after sewing so the ends are level. A plaited braid can be inserted through the fringe to make a tie at the front. If the top is slightly longer, this tie will cause the top to blouse out at the waist.

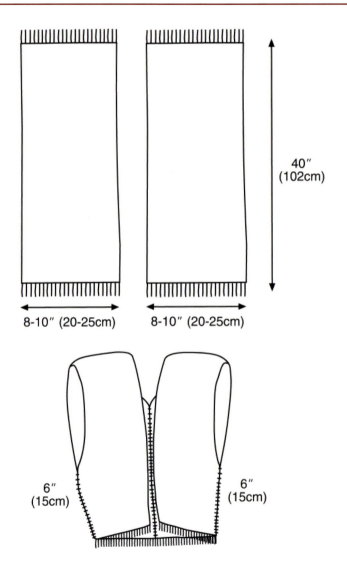

Figure 10-1. Straight top

Projects

Photo 10-1. Straight top

Collapse Weave

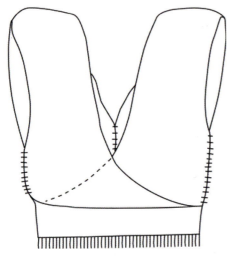

Figure 10-2. Mobius top

MOBIUS TOP

This is a simple top that drapes beautifully at the front. It is woven in one single strip and both ends are fringed. Weave a piece of fabric 8-10in (20-25cm) wide and 6 1/2 feet (195cm) long when finished. Fringe the ends before washing. These fringed ends will be at the lower back edge. To make the top, fold the length with the crossover section at the front. Pin or tack the seams so you can see how it hangs together before sewing. Join the center backs together for 10in (25cm) from the fringed ends. Join the side seams together for 5in (13cm). The illustrated top has a shorter front than back, with the back extending 5in (13cm) below the front to the waist. This leaves a good expanse of bare flesh showing: fine if you are an 18-year-old with a great figure. For those who prefer less skin showing, the front and back can be stitched to the same length. A stitch or two at the center front will hold the two edges together.

Photo 10-2. Mobius top

Collapse Weave

COCOON

This is another easy top to make and it drapes well in collapse fabric. Weave four lengths 35in (90cm) long and 8-10in (20-25cm) wide when finished. Fringe and wash. Hand sew one pair together for the full length, and repeat for the other pair. Then join the two pairs together at the center back for 21in (53cm). Fold the joined pairs in half lengthwise and sew the side seams together 5in (13cm) up from the fringe end to make the armhole.

Cocoons have always been popular with weavers, and a collapse cocoon will hang very well to make a shawl-like garment. When worn, the front neck edges turn back to make a collar.

Figure 10-3. Cocoon

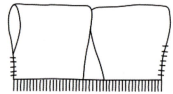

Projects

Photo 10-3. Cocoon

Collapse Weave

PANTS

To make baggy harem-type pants four lengths, 8-10in (20-25cm) wide and the appropriate length, can be joined together. Sew the center front and center back together for 13in (33cm) from the waist down. Then sew the side seams together. As these pants are baggy there is no need to cut the fabric in at the crutch; a straight join is all that is needed. The cuffs can be hemmed and a braid inserted to make them draw in at the ankle end, and the pants can then be allowed to hang loosely over the cuff. The waist can be hemmed and a braid inserted, or it can be sewn onto a band.

These pants are very comfortable to wear, and can be teamed up with any of the tops to make a complete outfit. The fringe can also be twisted and left as a decorative finish at either the cuff or waist end.

SKIRT

The fullness of the skirt is determined by the number of joined fabric strips. Four may be enough, or use five or six for a fuller skirt. The skirt can be gathered at the waist onto a band. Another option is to hem the waist edge then make a matching braid and insert it into the hem, gathering the fabric and forming a tie.

The lower edge can be fringed or over-sewn as described on Page 43 to make a wavy edge. As the skirt will need to be made in several lengths joined together, the joins can extend only part-way down the skirt length from the waist, leaving slits open to the knee. The fringe can be twisted and left as a decorative fringe at the waist or lower skirt end.

Photo 10-4. Pants with mobius top

Projects

Blue Dress. Woven by Anne Field, New Zealand.
56/2 over-twisted merino wool, 110/2 shrinkable
merino wool and acrylic yarns.
Dyed with fiber-reactive dyes.
Designed by Anne Field and Sylvia Campbell.
Photographer Edward Field.

Appendix

HAND SPINNING FOR COLLAPSE WEAVE

Many years ago, I was in a team in a 'fleece to garment' competition where teams had to spin the wool and knit a woolen jersey in the fastest possible time. While we were practicing it soon became clear that whenever my single yarn was plied with another spinner's yarn, the knitting 'skewed' off in a diagonal. Photo 3-3 shows the same effect, but this was not the result we were aiming for then. Eventually we worked out that my spinning wheel was putting more twist into the singles than my partner's wheel. My drive ratio was 11:1, hers was 7:1.

Drive ratio

Drive ratio is determined by the circumference of the drive wheel, divided by the circumference of the flyer or bobbin whorl. On a flyer-led wheel, drive ratio can be determined by tying a thread to one flyer arm then counting the number of times the flyer rotates to one turn of the drive wheel. On a bobbin-led wheel, mark a spot on the bobbin then count the number of times the bobbin rotates to one turn of the drive wheel. My wheel was putting 11 twists to the inch in the yarn, her wheel was putting in seven. When plied together, the yarn was not balanced. The solution was to spin on the same wheels, with the same drive ratios.

Balanced plied yarn

In handspinning, a balanced yarn is spun by taking two singles with the same twist count and plying them together. The ply twist count should be two-thirds of the twist of the singles with the twist in the opposite direction. When plying in the opposite direction, some of the original twist is undone, then more added, hence the two-thirds proportion.

Unbalanced plied yarn

Where two singles with different twist counts are plied together, as in my 'fleece to garment' example above, the yarn will be unbalanced. This also will happen when two singles yarns are plied with more or less than the two-thirds twist of the singles. For example, two singles each spun with six twists to the inch, then plied with eight or nine twists to the inch, will be over-twisted and unbalanced. To balance this yarn, it should be plied with four twists to the inch.

Any spinner who has taken an unbalanced yarn off a niddy noddy will have seen the effect when the twist in the singles does not balance the ply twist. The skein tries to straighten out and twists around itself.

Most spinners spin singles with a Z twist, with the wheel turning in a clockwise direction. Then they ply in an S direction with the wheel turning in an anti-clockwise direction. If there is too much twist in the spinning compared to the plying, the skein twists in an S direction, because the yarn tries to straighten itself. If there is too much twist in the plying compared to the spinning, the skein will twist in a Z direction.

For a flat fabric a balanced yarn is used, that is one with no twist in either direction. If this yarn is seen through a microscope, all the fibers will run straight and parallel with the yarn length. In a collapse weave fabric, some of the yarn is unbalanced. The unbalanced portions, if allowed enough space when relaxed, will move and spiral, forming pleats. A single yarn is always unbalanced, because the twist is in one direction.

To experiment with this effect, I spun some singles for the warp with plenty of twist and wove this yarn into two scarves as described on page 15 and shown in Photo 2-1. The yarn was not easy to handle because it twisted and curled back on itself at every opportunity. I left the singles yarn on the bobbin for a few days to help straighten out the worst kinks then wound the warp directly from the bobbins without washing it first.

Putting the warp on the loom was fun. When I took the warp off the mill the yarn corkscrewed back on itself. I wound the warp onto the warp beam through a raddle from back to front with a tight tension, which straightened the warp out. When I cut a warp end to thread through the heddles, the tension relaxed and the yarns spiraled and attempted to untwist. Because I wanted the twist to remain in the yarn, I resorted to strong sticky tape to keep them from untwisting. Cutting through one warp loop at a time, I secured one of the pair with tape, threaded the other through the correct heddle and dent, then quickly taped the end to the breast beam. A lot of sticky tape was used.

Once on the loom, with tight tension, the warp remained passive, but when I took it off the loom and washed it the yarn tried to spiral and curl once again, forming interesting pleats.

Collapse Weave

I spun half the yarn with an S twist, and half with a Z twist, putting each type of yarn in alternating 1-inch bands across the warp. As you can see from Photo 2-1, the different twist direction is evident.

To get the amount of twist I needed for collapse to happen, the yarn was spun fine with plenty of twist. A finer breed, such a Merino or Corriedale, will be easier to spin this way. These are breeds which have more crimps or waves and will spiral more easily than a coarser wool with fewer crimps. The yarn structure makes a difference too. Woolen yarns, spun with the fibers arranged haphazardly, shrinks more than a worsted-spun yarn, which has parallel fibers and is more solid in construction.

There are two ways you can use your spinning wheel to make over-twisted yarn. You can make your own yarn by spinning from the wool itself, as in Photo 2-1, or you can put commercial yarn through the spinning wheel to add more twist to a balanced yarn.

Adding twist to commercial yarn

Twist can be added to commercial yarn on the spinning wheel. Fine two-ply yarn seems to work the best. Determine the direction of the twist, then run the yarn from the cone or ball through the spinning wheel, adding twist in the same direction. Make sure you are consistent and spin with a set number of treadles of the wheel to each length fed onto the bobbin. I did this at a spinning day once and it was a full hour before anyone bothered to ask me what I was doing. I was counting under my breath the whole time to make sure I added the same amount of twist and it took some concentration. If the twist count is not the same for the weft yarn, the finished weaving will be wider at some points than others, something I found out to my irritation when I washed a piece of weaving. The sections where I had added less twist bulged out at the sides because that area had not collapsed as much as the rest of the weaving. Do not set the twist by washing the yarn after it has been re-spun. I leave it on the bobbin and wind my shuttles directly from the bobbin on a lazy kate.

Before I could buy commercial over-twisted yarn from the mills, adding twist like this was the only way, apart from spinning my own, that I could get suitable yarn for collapse weave.

Appendix

Spinning your own yarn for collapse weave

The simplest way is to spin a singles yarn, because this is always unbalanced. To make the twist consistent, count the number of treadles to each draft. Using the smallest whorl on your wheel will make it quicker because this whorl will have the highest drive ratio.

If the flyer turns six times to one turn of the drive wheel, your drive ratio is 6:1 and you are putting in six twists to one turn of the drive wheel. If you feed one inch of yarn onto the wheel for each turn of the drive wheel, there are six twists in that inch. If you feed two inches for two turns of the drive wheel, there will also be six twists per inch, and so on. You should count the number of treadles to each draft, to make sure the same number of twists are going into each draft length. The more twists in the singles, the more the collapse. A good guide is that if the yarn twists and curls on the bobbin, there is sufficient twist to cause collapse. Do not wash this yarn before weaving, because you want the twist to release and set in the fabric itself. It is easier to wind the shuttle straight from the bobbin.

When joining singles as you spin, make the join gradually tapered over several inches to both strengthen the yarn and to keep it more even, particularly if it is being used as a warp yarn.

When weaving with this yarn as a weft, the yarn kinks as the shuttle lays it across the shed. I found an end-delivery shuttle straightened the yarn out better than any other shuttle, as the slight amount of drag on the weft straightened it out for me. Over-twisted yarn purchased from a mill seems to be more manageable than yarn I have over-twisted on the spinning wheel, perhaps because the commercial yarn has been wound tightly onto a cone or some other type of holder and has remained on the holder for some time.

The advantage with spinning your own over-twist wool is that you have complete control over the process. You can choose your own fleece, knowing that a soft Merino fleece will shrink more than a coarser breed such as Romney. You can spin it worsted, for less shrinkage, or woolen for more collapse. You can add exactly the twist count you want. The disadvantage is that it is a slow, repetitive process. I have been known to fall asleep while spinning like this.

List of Suppliers

Wool singles, 26 wraps per inch
Alpaca singles, 20 wraps per inch
These yarns were custom spun for me.
Tai Tapu Wool Carders,
53 Main Akaroa Highway,
Tai Tapu, New Zealand.
Fax 03 329 6889

Tencel 10/2, 8/2
Webs Service Center,
P.O.Box 147, Northhampton, MA, USA.
Ph 01061-0147
www.webs@yarn.com

Halcyon Yarn
12 School Street, Bath, ME 04530, USA.
email: slu@halcyonyarn.com

110/2 shrinkable merino
Glenora Craft, Pleasant Place, Dunedin,
New Zealand.
email: glenora@paradise.net.nz

Over-twisted Merino wool
Anne Field, 37 Rhodes St, Christchurch 8014, New Zealand.
email: afield@chch.planet.org.nz

1/30 wool over-twisted yarn
This yarn is described in the catalog as wool crepe and comes in many colors.

Habu Textiles, 135 West 29th St, Suite 403,
New York City, New York, 10001, USA.
www.habutextiles.com

20/2 mulberry silk
Walters Import, 449 Beaudesert Rd, Moorooka, 4105
Queensland, Australia.
Fax 07 3841 3514

20/2 Bombyx silk
Yarn Barn of Kansas
930 Massachusetts, Lawrence, KS 66044, USA.
www.yarnbarn-ks.com

Wool crepe
Colored, Z and S over-twisted yarn is available from the Danish Yarn Purchasing Association (GIF). This yarn measures 30,000m/kg. To purchase yarn you need to become a member of this organization. For details go to:
www.yarn.dk

Stretch wool and superwash wool yarns
Dea Nominees Ltd.
Supplier of 5 colors of stretch wool, superwash wool yarns, nylon/Lycra.
email: horowhenua@optus.net.au
www.deayarns.com.au

Halcyon Yarns - email: slu@halcyonyarn.com

Yarn Barn - www.yarnbarn-ks.com

Possum/Merino yarn

Glenora Weaving Supplies, P. O. Box 9 Gerrongong, NSW 2534, Australia.
Phone/Fax 02 4234 0422
email:Christine@GlenoraWeaving.com.au
www.GlenoraWeaving.com.au
Although this source is Australian, the yarn originates in New Zealand from:
Quality Yarns, 1 Edward St, Milton,
New Zealand.
email: qualityarns@xtra.co.nz

1/26 wool

Humphries Weaving Company Ltd, DeVere Mill, Queen St, Castle Hedingham, Halstead. Essex, CO9 3HA UK.
www.humphriesweaving.co.uk

Elastic yarns

Yarn Barn, 200 Reynard St, West Coburg,
VIC 3058, Australia.
Ph 03 9386 0361 Fax 03 9386 0542

Colcolastic

Venne Cocoton Unikat, Eyserheide 35, 6287 NB Eys/Witten, The Netherlands.
email: sales@vennecolcoton.com
www.vennecolcoton.com

Louet, 808 Commerce Park Drive, Ogdensburg, NY 13669, USA.
email: info@louet.com
www.louet.com

Agnes Hauptli, 827 Oruru Road, RD 2, Kaitaia 0482, New Zealand.
email: ahauptli@orcon.net.nz
www.fiberholics.orcon.net.nz
She also sells black Elastotwist and over-twisted rayon S and Z twist.

20/2 Cotton/Lycra yarn

Textura Trading Company
www.texturatrading.com

Bibliography

Alderman, Sharon. 'Tracking the Mystery of the Crinkling Cloth' *Handwoven*, Sept/Oct 1985, pp. 31-33.

Clark, Amy C. 'Organic Structure: The Art of Overtwist With Ann Richards'. *Handwoven* November/December 1996, pp. 32-34.

Dalaard, Lotte. 'Magiske Materialer'. Published 2007, Forlaget Fiberfeber, Denmark

De Ruiter, Erica. 'Scarves in Diagonal Pleats'. *Weaver's*, Fall 1997, pp. 40-41.

Durant, Judith. Project Editor. *Handwoven Scarves* Interweave Press, CO, USA 1999.

Elliot, Lillian. 'In Search of Collapse', *In Celebration of the Curious Mind*. Interweave Press, 1983, pp. 103-109.

Field, Anne. 'Collapse-Weave Scarf'. *Handwoven* September/October 2004, pp. 48-50.

Frame, Mary. 'Ringlets and Waves: Undulations From Over-twist' *Spin-Off* Winter 1986, pp. 28-33

Frame, Mary. 'Save the Twist, Warping and Weaving With Over-twisted Yarns' *Spin-Off* June 1987.

Hochberg, Bette. 'Add a New twist to Your Spinning'. *Spin-Off,* 1981, pp. 42-45.

Inouye, Bonnie. 'Pointed Furrows'. *Weaver's,* Fall 1997, pp. 42-43.

Inouye, Bonnie. 'Furrowed Scarves'. *Weaver's,* Fall 1997, pp. 45

Quinn, Celia. 'Experimenting with Silk Crepe', *Spin-Off* Winter 1986, pp. 36-37.

Richards, Ann. 'Breaking Into Waves. *Handwoven* November/December 1996, pp. 33-38

Rude, Sandra. 'Collapse Scarves'. *Weaver's,* Fall 1997, pp. 46-47.

Ruiter, Erica de. 'Scarves in Diagonal Pleats'. *Weaver's,* Fall 1997, pp. 40-41.

Sekimachi, Kay. 'Collapse In Double and Plain Weave'. *Weaver's,* Fall 1997, pp. 48-49.

Van der Hoogt, Madelyn. Morrison, Ruth. Field, Anne. Van der Wel, Marjolyn. 'A Perplexing Plethora of Pleats'. *Weaver's,* Fall 1997, pp. 34-39.

Van der Hoogt, Madelyn, Ed. *The Best of Weaver's : Fabrics That Go Bump*. Published 2002, XRX Inc., Sioux Falls, USA.

Watson, William. *Textile Design and Colour* Fifth edition published 1946. Longman, Green & Co. Ltd, London. pp. 14-16.

More titles for Weavers and Knitters by Anne Field

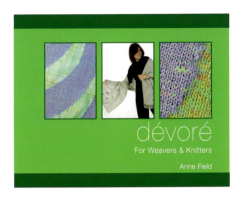

Dévoré For Weavers & Knitters by Anne Field
Dévoré is a process that has been used in the fashion industry for many years. Originally it was known as "poor man's lace" and was called "broderie chimique" in Europe because it was used to simulate machine embroidery. The main use of dévoré has been on cut velvet fabric with a pile of viscose or rayon on a silk backing. The rayon was burnt out leaving elaborate etched patterns on the transparent silk backing.
Dévoré, from the French word for devour, is the process where sodium bisulphate is applied to cloth which is then dried and heated. The heat causes the sodium bisulphate to eat away at the fabric, leaving the treated area transparent. This book shows you how to make the cloth for dévoré, the solution and the process to make your own beautiful dévoré fabrics.

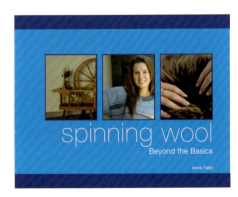

Spinning Wool: Beyond the Basics by Anne Field
This book is intended for spinners who have mastered the basic spinning techniques explored in The Ashford Book of Spinning. First it shows spinners how to analyse a fleece on its own merits and includes many examples of fleece types from all over the world. The functions of bobbin and flyer wheels are discussed in detail, and how to make the most of a wide range of wheel types, including Timbertops, Ashford, Louet, Schacht and Majacraft.
The yarn design section of the book takes spinners step-by-step through the process of spinning yarns of a pre-determined size and twist count, and shows how to spin everthing from solid hard-wearing worsted to soft, fluffy woollen yarns. Also included are projects that suggest suitable end uses for handspun yarn.

For further information, please contact Anne Field by email or via her website.
email: afield@chch.planet.org.nz   or visit: www.annefield.co.nz

Index

A
acrylic 25, 39, 41, 149
active 3, 8, 11, 14, 17, 20, 24, 34, 35, 37, 42, 43, 45, 66
Adding twist to commercial yarn 152
ADVANCING TWILL 137
alpaca 26, 109, 111, 120
angle of twist 19, 22

B
balanced 14, 20, 24, 27, 28, 34, 45, 97, 104, 109, 125, 127, 150, 151, 152
Basket weave 4, 106, 125, 126
bouclé 11, 37, 109

C
Calculating Twist 21
COCOON 146
colcolastic 119, 141
Color sequence 3, 52
commercial yarns 15, 19, 24
Contrast areas 3, 54
Corriedale 24, 152
Cotton 25, 141
crepe 22, 38, 39, 75, 154
cross sticks 67, 69, 70, 71
crows' feet 26

D
DEFLECTED DOUBLE WEAVE 107
DIAGONAL TWILL 132
Double Weave 72-93
drafts
    Explanation of 13
Drive ratio 150
Dyeing 45, 141

E
EIGHT-SHAFT DOUBLE WEAVE 82
Elastic 24, 33, 155
elastomeric yarn 33
energized 24
English Leicester 7, 24
Exchanging two layers 3, 4, 76, 77, 85, 87
EXCHANGING VERTICAL LAYERS 89

F
FELTED FLOATS 124
felting 4, 7, 64, 111
Finishing 3, 62
    floats 25, 31, 32, 46, 64, 78, 79, 86, 88, 95, 97, 114, 115, 116, 117, 118, 124, 125, 126
four-shaft double weave 72, 82
fringe finishes 43
fulling 6, 7

G
GATHERED SQUARES 119
GATHERING 112

H
Habu Textiles 22, 154
HAND SPINNING 150
handspun 6, 9, 13, 15, 24, 157
heddles 67, 68, 70, 71, 73, 96, 151
hem stitching 43
HUCKABACK 132

I
Italian diamond 4, 130, 132

K

knitting 27, 150, 157

L

light reflection 16
linen 24, 41, 45
linsey-woolsey 41
luster 22
Lycra 12, 31, 33, 45, 49, 53, 54, 55, 88, 96, 97, 114, 117, 119, 127, 129, 130, 131, 132, 133, 154
Lyocell. *See* Tencel

M

mercerized 25, 37, 112
Merino 7, 24, 89, 106, 107, 125, 128, 152, 153, 154
micron 21, 24
milling 6
Miniature Monk's belt 4, 130
MOBIUS TOP 144
mohair 20, 37, 58, 112

N

non-energized 24

O

one-shuttle weave 97
OVERSHOT WEAVE 128

P

PANTS 148
passive 3, 8, 17, 20, 24, 25, 34, 35, 38, 42, 50, 66, 151
PASSIVE YARNS 34, 36
Pick-up weaving 80, 81, 91
plain weave 9, 26, 28, 31, 38, 46, 54, 57, 60, 72, 82, 89, 109, 118,
pleating 12, 27, 47, 50, 51, 52, 54, 57, 62, 64, 88, 104, 117, 140
plying 14, 150, 151
possum/merino blend yarn 106

R

raddle 3, 66, 67, 69, 70, 151
Rayon 7
reed 6, 50, 67, 68, 70, 73, 79, 80, 114, 118
Reversing the layers 4, 90
ribbon 112, 114
ripple edge 43

S

SAMPLE A 17
SAMPLE B 28
SAMPLE C 31
SAMPLE D 48
SAMPLE E 55, 59, 61
SAMPLE F 59
SAMPLE G 61
S and Z twist 14, 155
SCARVES 141
sectional warping 66
seersucker 7, 11
selvedge 30, 67, 77, 83, 96, 108, 124
sett 27, 35, 36, 45, 50, 104, 109, 124,
shrinkage 7, 24, 25, 26, 43, 104, 106, 125, 141, 153
SHUTTLES 13, 153
singles 14, 15, 21, 22, 23, 26, 109, 150, 151, 153, 154
SIXTEEN-SHAFT TWILL 91
SKIRT 148
SPACED WARP AND WEFT 118
spinning 13, 14, 15, 21, 22, 24, 150, 151, 152, 153, 157
Spinning your own yarn 153
steaming method 42

Straight draw 112
STRAIGHT TOP 142
structure 6, 7, 8, 14, 46
SUPPLEMENTARY WARPS 94
SWEDISH LACE 127
synthetic yarns 25

T
tabby binder 128
Tencel 25, 105, 107, 108, 112, 120, 154
Testing yarn 41
Tex 17, 22, 23, 42
tracking 26, 76, 109, 111
Tussah silk 25
twelve-shaft
double weaves 84
twill
    3/1 & 1/3
        8, 9, 47, 48, 50, 54, 84, 112

    2/2
        8, 9, 82, 100, 112
twists per inch 22
two warp beams 3, 68, 72, 73

W
waffle weave 25, 47
Warp collapse 36, 57
warp-faced 9, 47, 49, 50
warp from back to front 66
warping board 3, 66
warping mill 3, 66
WARPS OVER 15 FEET 70
Washing 6, 17, 35, 43, 64
Weaving a tube 3, 4, 74, 75, 76, 77, 82
Weft collapse 37
weft-face 8, 9, 52, 134
Width of the stripes 50

woolen 7, 9, 24, 25, 150, 153
worms 30, 129
Worsted 24
WRAPS 142
wraps per inch 12, 104, 109, 154

Y
Yarn 3, 6, 7, 14, 24, 34, 50, 154, 155
YARN HANDLE 21
YARN NAMING 22
Yarn size 3, 34, 50